OUR BEST COOKBOOK

2

A Second Serving

*A collection of fine recipes
submitted by members of the
Wisconsin Restaurant Association.*

Wisconsin Restaurant Association Education Foundation
Madison, Wisconsin

First edition

ISBN: 0-942495-47-0

Library of Congress Catalog Card Number: 95-61352

Wisconsin Restaurant Association Education Foundation
31 South Henry Street, Suite 300
Madison, Wisconsin 53703

For additional copies of this book, contact:
    Amherst Press
    318 N Main Street
    PO Box 296
    Amherst, Wisconsin 54406
    or call 1-800-333-8122

Printed in the United States of America by:
    Palmer Publications, Inc.
    Amherst, Wisconsin 54406

Back cover photographs by Nicholas Patrinos

WISCONSIN RESTAURANT ASSOCIATION EDUCATION FOUNDATION

1995-96 BOARD OF DIRECTORS

President: Mike Pitzo
Vice President: Kathleen Cullen
Treasurer: George Krug
Secretary/Executive Officer: Ed Lump
WRA President: Rollin Natter

James Alevizos
Mark Andrea
Knut Apitz
Steve Becker
Mary Jane Best-Louther
LeRoy Bochler
Bill Boelter
James Buergermeister, Ph.D.
Jim Cornelius
Russell Fetting
Heinz Fischer
Al Gagliano
Pamela Gottsacker
Ron Heuser
Tim Horan
Bernard Kurzawa
Joe LoPiparo
Susan Quam
Dick Radell
John Roherty
Mary Rowley
Richard Rupp
Ron Speich
Robert Spindell, Jr.
Michelle Steinbrecher
Mike Stone
Ward Torke
Bruce Weegman

Jeffrey Igel, Senior Director
Gail Parr, Executive Director of Operations
Sally Scott, Director of Development
Kristy Bouchie, Director of Programs
Becky Boettcher, Administrative Assistant

CONTENTS

ACKNOWLEDGMENTS

It is with great pleasure that we bring you the second edition of Our Best Cookbook.

Warm thanks to the good folks who took time out of their busy schedules to share recipes. We appreciate the effort it takes to convert a recipe for 80 to a recipe for 8! A special thanks to Paul and Sara Bancroft-Short, owners of the lovely Sandhill Inn, Merrimac, who most graciously shared their photo which became the cover for this book (recipe on page 115).

We are most pleased to have the Wisconsin Milk Marketing Board as our sponsor of Our Best Cookbook 2. Wisconsin has a proud tradition of the best in dairy products. Our member restaurants cook for you using the finest of ingredients beginning with these wonderful products.

Thank you to Bob Wollersheim and Wollersheim Winery, Prairie du Sac.

Please enjoy trying new recipes, reading a bit about our scholarship students, and touring our beautiful state while discovering old favorites and wonderful new restaurants in which to dine.

Sally Scott

Sally Scott
Director of Development

Welcome to Wisconsin's fine dining.

Wisconsin is a beautiful state, blessed with many opportunities
for those who work and play here. One of Wisconsin's most unique
offerings is its fine dining. We here in Wisconsin host some of
the finest restaurants in the world, and as President of the
Wisconsin Restaurant Association Education Foundation,
I encourage you to visit our member establishments.

Since it is not possible to visit all of our fine restaurants,
the Wisconsin Restaurant Association Education Foundation
is offering you a chance to try some of Wisconsin's best cuisine,
first-hand, by publishing a collection of your favorite recipes
from Wisconsin's best dining establishments.

I encourage you to try these wonderful recipes and visit Wisconsin
Restaurant Association member restaurants. I know you won't
be disappointed.

Sincerely,

Michael F. Pitzo
President

SCHOLARSHIPS IN FOODSERVICE

Proceeds from the sale of this book will go toward the Wisconsin Restaurant Association Education Foundation Scholarship Program.

Each year the Education Foundation awards scholarships of $750 to $1500 to twenty or more students. These students are training in a variety of foodservice career paths. They may be enrolled in a one-, two-, or four-year program or a food-service apprenticeship program. The student must be employed in a Wisconsin food-service position at the time of application.

The Education Foundation also participates in a special needs scholarship program for foodservice students through the vocational technical colleges. Other grants and support are given as the need arises, such as money donated to help the Future Homemakers of America Home Economics Related Occupations (FHA-HERO) students attend their national conferences. Since 1983, the Foundation has awarded over $130,000 in scholarships, grants and aids.

Anyone interested in this program or other Education Foundation endeavors is welcome to contact Kristy Bouchie, Director of Programs, 800-589-3211.

1995 EDUCATION FOUNDATION SCHOLARSHIP RECIPIENTS

Sheila Applen
Wisconsin Indianhead Technical College
Foodservice Management Program, Second Year

Sheila wants to use her 20 years of experience in the foodservice industry and schooling to pursue her goal of owning and operating her own business. "As a non-traditional student, I see higher education as a privilege and am excited to be involved in it."

Instructor Victor Bagan gives Sheila much credit. "She has shown a mature approach to school work, and is helpful to other students. When asked to help, she is always dependable."

Ginger Baker
MATC-Milwaukee
Culinary Apprentice Program, Second Year
Sponsored by Adolph Brettschneider

Ginger, a student member of the American Culinary Federation, believes that the largest challenge in the foodservice industry is "how to maintain a high level of creativity while still bringing in a profit that will keep you in business."

Axel Dietrich, executive chef of The Grand Milwaukee Hotel, believes Ginger to be extremely qualified to continue the formal academic rigors in the culinary arts program. "She possesses the interest, motivation, and excitement necessary to continue her academic career and, more importantly, she has the discipline to successfully finish the program and apply what she's learned and experienced to the world she touches."

Thomas Boivin
Fox Valley Technical College-Appleton
Culinary Arts Program, First Year
Sponsored by Edward Don & Company

Thomas has over 10 years experience in the foodservice industry. "I chose this industry because of the satisfaction I get from preparing gourmet meals, elegant banquets, and even a home-cooked meal."

Employer Fred Doyle, of Forest Island restaurant in Keshena, rates Thomas as exceptional. "He is constantly striving to become more creative and expand his culinary skills. The skills and knowledge he is learning, he passes on to the other staff members on a constant and daily basis."

Peter Bothe
MATC-Madison
Culinary Arts Program, First Year
Sponsored by Wisconsin Gas Company

Peter plans to attend a culinary academy. "I want to work as a chef in an elegant restaurant." Peter also has plans of owning his own restaurant.

Peter's employer, Kelly Seidel, of the Pine Cone restaurant in Johnson Creek, gives him high ratings. "He shows a great deal of leadership with the rest of the staff. He is an important asset to my staff."

Jason Damrow
Moraine Park Technical College
Culinary Arts Program, Second Year
Sponsored by Miller Brewing Company

Jason competed in the 1995 WRA Student Culinary Competition and earned a silver medal. "I want a career in foodservice because I like to cook and it interests me a lot."

Norine McGaw of NoNo's restaurant in Milwaukee, made the following recommendation: "Jason is probably the most unique young person I have ever met. Jason sets the pace in the kitchen. By his example, others in the kitchen are much more productive when he works."

Susan Ellis
Western Wisconsin Technical College
Foodservice Management, Second Year
Sponsored by Ocean Spray Cranberries, Inc.

Susan is co-owner of Celebration Creation working in all areas from food prep and baking to bookkeeping. "I love the foodservice business! I cannot possibly believe there is any other field that could challenge and fulfill me. This is definitely the career for my future."

Deborah Klug, Susan's instructor, believes Susan to be academically superior in her foodservice classes. "I believe that her greatest asset is her sense of humility and her constant pursuit of the 'better way.' It is refreshing to work with a person that is able to share her mistakes as well as triumphs."

Russell Gorski
MATC-Milwaukee
Culinary Arts Program, First Year
Sponsored by Wisconsin River Valley Chapter of the WRA and Neesvigs

Russell works at Pinewood Supper Club as a cook. "One of the major challenges in the industry would be keeping up with the new techniques that come about from different parts of the world."

Steven Allen of Pinewood Supper Club nominates Russell as an excellent candidate for our scholarship. "He is a very hard working young individual. His interest in the foodservice industry is surpassed by none."

Isaac Greenwood
MATC-Madison
Culinary Arts Program, First Year

Isaac is employed by the General Store as a dishwasher and cook. "I think the most important challenge in the foodservice industry is employee relations. When improving employee relations you gain their respect and loyalty."

Employer Todd Miller, of Spring Green General Store, nominated Isaac. "Isaac shows a great interest in his job and exhibits a willingness to learn and expand his job duties."

Jeffrey Greif
Nicolet Area Technical College
Culinary Arts Program, Second Year

Jeffrey works at the Hiawatha Supper Club in Eagle River as an assistant to the chef. "I like cooking and serving the public while making their meals enjoyable. I would like to join the American Culinary Federation and further my education."

Instructor Linda Arndt believes Jeffrey to be a natural in the kitchen. "He is willing to try new approaches to food production and is eager to learn." Jeffrey was chosen to represent the Nicolet Culinary Program at the National Restaurant Association's Salute to Excellence.

George Kalka
University of Wisconsin-Stout
Hospitality & Tourism Management, First Year
Sponsored by WRA Purveyors/Ginny Atkins

George is intrigued by the foodservice industry. "An appreciation for each customer as an individual has helped me to relate and communicate with them. The foodservice industry is a way of life for me and I have a true passion for the business."

George is presently employed by Pedro's Mexican Restaurante in Wisconsin Dells as a work release student. Marcia Morris, Manager Trainee, states: "I know that he will be a candidate that the Wisconsin Restaurant Association Education Foundation would be proud to select to receive this scholarship, because George will be a great leader for the restaurant business in the future."

William Libby
Moraine Park Technical College
Culinary Arts Program, Second Year

William is presently working at Carvers on the Lake, Green Lake, as a cook. He finds foodservice to be a rewarding career. "I like the fast pace, and the opportunity it gives me to be creative."

Employer Mary Marks praises William's work. "Through his first semester of school at MPTC I can see Bill gaining the confidence to try new ideas and offer his suggestions. He has always offered us total commitment of himself as an employee and I can see this coming through as a culinary arts student."

Timothy Marks
University of Wisconsin-Stout
Hospitality & Tourism Management/Culinary Arts Program, First Year
Sponsored by Torke Coffee Roasting Company

Timothy enjoys being creative with foods and recipes. "I love my job; working with food, being creative, but also working so closely with people—both co-workers and the public."

Employers Robert and Kathy Jo Kokott of Inn the Olden Days, Mukwonago, rate Timothy as exceptional. "Tim is a very dedicated and conscientious employee of ours. Tim's creativity in the kitchen has resulted with several different new menu ideas and daily specials for our restaurants."

Jane Matthews
Fox Valley Technical College-Appleton
Culinary Arts Program, Second Year

Jane competed in the 1995 WRA Student Culinary Competition and claimed a bronze medal. She will also be representing her school for the Salute to Excellence Award. Regarding career goals, Jane says she will: "Keep my mind, ears, and eyes open to new experiences and opportunities that would be of interest."

Instructor Helen Dean made the following recommendation: "Her spirit and excitement for learning and doing has spilled over onto fellow students to whom she is always willing to give a helping hand. She is ready to volunteer when extra duty is called for in school activities, and the jobs are always well done."

Kathleen Mayenschein
Chippewa Valley Technical College
Culinary Arts Program, First Year

Kathleen desires a position as a cook or other aspects of the food industry. "I believe the need for foodservice facilities and workers will continue to rapidly increase into the future as people eat away from home more and more."

Instructor Janice Verhulst of Thorp High School notes that Kathleen has been a very active member of FHA/HERO as well as other organizations. "She has demonstrated her ability to work with people and be a leader, both in the classroom and on her own."

Fredrick "Chuck" Meitner
Mid-State Technical College
Culinary Apprenticeship, Second Year

Chuck is presently working as a cook at Bernard's in Stevens Point. "I want a career in foodservice because I love the challenge of cooking. I can think of nothing better than to do this the rest of my life."

Employer Bernard Kurzawa nominated Chuck with high praises. "He is very much committed to his profession. I feel Chuck has what it takes to be an excellent chef."

Denise Mikalowsky
University of Wisconsin-Stout
Hospitality & Tourism Management, Fourth Year
Sponsored by Superior Coffee

Denise is interested in researching new foodservice technology and environmental concerns. "I am pursuing a career in foodservice because I hope to reach a level where I may bring changes in our industry concerning nutrition awareness, waste management, and recycling issues."

Employer Daniel Thomas, of Randall's Riverfront in Sheboygan, believes Denise to be very dedicated to her profession. "Denise Mikalowsky has dedicated herself to her future in the restaurant business." He also notes her devotion to customer service.

Kathryn Moe
Western Wisconsin Technical College
Foodservice Management, Second Year
Sponsored by Kennedy & Associates

As co-owner of Celebration Creations, Kathryn spends time in all areas from baking to purchasing. "Foodservice is what I know and do best. I believe service and quality go hand in hand and should be the number one priority of all foodservice people."

Instructor Deborah Klug nominated Kathryn as a deserving student for a foodservice scholarship. "Not only does Katie possess the people skills necessary to succeed in this service industry, but she also possesses intelligence, problem-solving skills, an eagerness to learn and achieve along with an incredible wealth of experience. I predict a high degree of success for Katie."

Betty Poff
Western Wisconsin Technical College
Foodservice Management, Second Year
Sponsored by Wisconsin Beef Council

Betty currently works at Coffee Cup Cafe in Bangor as a short order cook. It is the artistic side of her that is attracted to this creative field. "I get a personal sense of satisfaction from giving people something that I have created, that they will enjoy and that I will receive a positive feedback from doing.

Her employer, Larna Warthan, expressed how she wishes Betty could have been with her when she first opened. "Betty is a sweet, personable person dedicated to her choice of profession."

Chad Revoir
Chippewa Valley Technical College
Culinary Arts & Hospitality Management, Second Year

Chad, also a participant in the 1995 WRA Student Culinary Competition, earned himself a bronze medal. He enjoys using his artistic ability to create appealing dishes. "I've always wanted to be an artist and foodservice allows me to do so."

Instructor Paul Waters is pleased with Chad's excitement in the hospitality industry. "He is a very dedicated student who works hard to challenge the class and myself. I would hire this young man in a minute."

Eric Robinson
Culinary Institute of America
Culinary Arts Program, First Year

Eric works at Heritage House in Delavan as a cook. He has been cooking since he was very young and enjoys it a lot. "For a while now I've dreamed of being a chef who is able to be artistic in my own restaurant."

Andrew Drefs, Eric's employer, feels he is highly qualified and deserving of a scholarship award. "He has continued to work hard at improving his skills and the overall success of our operation." He considers Eric to be dedicated to his career.

Erin Sauer
Waukesha County Technical College
Culinary Management, Second Year
Sponsored by Elan Financial Services

Erin is currently Treasurer of the Junior American Culinary Federation at her school. "I want a career in the foodservice industry because I have a lifelong interest in food preparation. I find the industry to be very exciting and diverse in its opportunities."

Erin's employer, Michael Engel of Tripoli Country Club in Milwaukee, nominated her with high marks. "I really enjoy having Erin on my staff and hope that she remains here for a long time. She's earned the respect of the people she works with, which in this particular kitchen, means everything."

Adam Schroeder
Fox Valley Technical College
Restaurant Cook Apprenticeship, First Year

Adam has worked as a cook and is currently employed at Dairy Queen. He enjoys cooking and preparing food. To meet the challenge of preparing healthy, reasonably priced food that looks good and still earns a profit, Adam intends to learn the health benefits of different foods and innovative methods of preparation.

Edward Dory nominated Adam based on his responsible and dependable attitude towards work. "He is always willing to learn other tasks and takes on more work. I know he will do well in the foodservice industry."

Vicki Sims
Fox Valley Technical College
Culinary Arts Program, Second Year
Sponsored by Threshermen's Mutual Insurance Company

Vicki is currently employed at Embassy Suites in Green Bay, as a saute and pantry chef. "I feel very proud when I have prepared a delicious meal and have the talent to also make the meal a work of art." She feels a career in culinary arts will be very satisfying.

Employer Scott Nei gives Vicki an exceptional rating. "Vicki has expressed the strongest desire to achieve and learn as much as possible in many areas of our kitchen." Scott sees Vicki as an artist with the ability to manage.

Nancy Vaughan
Midstate Technical College
Food and Hospitality Management, Second Year

Nancy has always found excitement working in restaurants. "I know that the foodservice industry provides unlimited avenues and advancement opportunities. To go to work everyday and enjoy it is why I have chosen to prepare for a career in foodservice."

Stephen McNeely, a former employer from Village Plaza in Spencer, nominated her. "Nancy was like a breath of fresh air. She was dedicated to her job, trustworthy, always busy. She knew how to handle people and she was a good leader."

Amy Yogerst
Moraine Park Technical College
Culinary Arts Program, Second Year
Sponsored by Adolf Brettschneider

Amy wants a career in foodservice because she enjoys food preparation. She received the Moraine Park Vocational award for the culinary arts program, and is active in the Foodservice Executives Club.

According to her employer, David Polster of Top of the Ridge in West Bend, Amy strives to improve her abilities and knowledge. "She has shown since the first day that she wants to be in foodservice. I personally feel that with her dedication to this field, she will become a very successful restaurant operator."

MAKE IT WISCONSIN CHEESE
from the dairy farm families of Wisconsin

Wisconsin dairy products are traditional and integral to the taste-tempting foods served in homes and restaurants across the state. Wisconsin is famous for fresh milk, creamy butter and award-winning cheese—more than 300 varieties, types and styles of cheese. That special dairy heritage began over 150 years ago, when European immigrants discovered that the state's lush pasture land and clean water were ideal for dairying and began producing plentiful supplies of wholesome milk. Soon old-world cheesemasters established plants here to make cheeses from their homeland as well as new varieties. Wisconsin became the country's top cheese producer and a leader in establishing stringent quality standards, such as grading cheese for quality and requiring cheesemaker licensing. Those high standards, the old-world cheese artistry and modern-day technology together form the foundation of Wisconsin's continued role as a dairy industry leader. That leading role is enriched as descendants of those early immigrants and more recently arrived cheesemakers from Italy, Switzerland, France, and Germany make more varieties of specialty cheese from America's Dairyland. Here's a look at just a few of the cheese varieties that are made in Wisconsin, the legacy of generations of cheesemaking expertise:

Elegant **Brie** and **Camembert** are flat, round-shaped, rich and creamy-tasting cheeses covered with distinctive, white, "bloomy rind," an edible mold.

Blue cheese is a piquant, full-flavored cheese known for the blue mold that provides its flavor. Blue is native to France; **Gorgonzola** is an Italian-style Blue that is made here and is available in crumbly and creamy styles.

Immigrant German cheesemakers introduced **Muenster** to Wisconsin; it is a mild, creamy cheese often identified by its orange rind, although it can be made without it.

Limburger, of Belgian origin, is known for its pungent aroma, although its flavor is surprisingly mild and creamy when the rind is trimmed away. Wisconsin has the only Limburger plant in the entire country.

Delightful **Gouda** and **Edam** are buttery, nutty cheeses that are round and covered in wax; red wax suggests mild cheese, yellow or clear wax indicates aged or flavored cheese, and brown wax suggests smoked cheese.

Famous **Swiss** has distinctive "eyes" and a nutty, mellow flavor. Swiss cheesemakers brought other varieties to Wisconsin, as well, such as **Gruyere**, similar to Swiss but without holes and with a fuller flavor, and **Raclette**, served by scraping off layers of warmed cheese and eating the soft cheese atop boiled potatoes and other vegetables.

Cheddar, which was first made in England, is America's favorite cheese flavor. It can be made as a white or golden-hued cheese; its flavor becomes more complex and pleasingly sharp with age.

The Italians contributed an array of cheeses to Wisconsin. Some Italian-style cheeses have distinctive, stretchy qualities, such as *Mozzarella*, favored as pizza cheese, and *Provolone*, which has a more complex flavor. Grana cheeses are often aged for a nutty/sharp flavor and hard texture, and include grating cheeses such as *Parmesan*, *Romano* and *Asiago*. Full-flavored *Fontina* is a versatile cheese that becomes firm-textured with age. Zesty *Pepato* is Romano cheese with whole black peppercorns dispersed throughout. Fresh Italian-style cheeses include *Fresh Mozzarella*, which has a mild delicate flavor, *Ricotta*, a creamy-white, granular cheese that's mild and slightly sweet, and *Mascarpone*, a soft, creamy, buttery-flavored cheese that's used in sauces and desserts.

Greek cheesemakers brought their specialties to Wisconsin: distinctively tart and salty *Feta* and *Kasseri*, white cheeses with firm, crumbly textures that enliven salads and other dishes.

Wisconsin cheesemakers also produce Hispanic-style cheeses such as *Asadero*, a yellow-tinted cheese that melts without separating, and *Queso Quesadilla*, a white cheese with the same characteristics. *Anejo Enchilado* is a full-flavored, firm cheese rolled in paprika. *Cotija* is a dry, hard cheese known as the "Parmesan of Mexico." Several fresh Hispanic-style cheeses are made: *Queso Fresco* is soft and fine-grained, while *Queso Blanco* is crumbly; both hold their texture and shape when cooked. *Crema Mexicana* is a fresh rich-tasting cheese that's smooth, thick and pourable.

The state's skilled cheesemakers also make cheeses native to the Middle East. *Ackawi*, originally from Lebanon and Syria, is a smooth-textured, salty white cheese. *Paneer*, native to Iran and India, is available in two varieties: one has no added salt for sweet applications, while the other has a bit of added salt and is used with curries and in fried dough. *Basket Cheese* is a white, soft cheese formed in a basket. *Tuma*, native to Armenia, is a white, open-textured, mild-tasting fresh cheese, while *Kashta* is a rich-tasting, fresh cream product.

Original cheese varieties have been created by Wisconsin cheesemakers over the years: Versatile *Brick* has a distinctive, slightly nutty flavor that becomes pungent with age. Deliciously mild *Colby* has a golden color and smooth texture. Spreadable *Cold Pack* is a soft, creamy mixture of natural cheeses blended without heat; its appearance and texture are similar to the cheese from which it's made.

Wisconsin cheesemakers use special techniques to create taste-tempting cheese flavors, colors and textures: *Marbled cheese* is a familiar example; two cheese varieties or colors are blended, such as golden Colby and creamy-white Monterey Jack. *Smoking* also adds intriguing dimensions in flavor and color to cheeses such as Cheddar, Swiss, Provolone, Mozzarella, and Gouda. *Added ingredients and flavorings*

result in exciting cheese options such as Havarti with dill, Cheddar with bacon, Muenster with cranberries, Brie with herbs, Feta with sun-dried tomatoes and basil, Monterey Jack with pesto, and Colby
with jalapeno peppers. *Special packaging* makes cheese fun and easy to eat. For example, many varieties
of cheese, including String cheese, a form of Mozzarella, are available individually packaged in stick
form, so they're ideal for lunches or snacks on the go. And a wide variety of convenience cheese forms
are made, including blends of two or more cheese varieties, such as a classic four-cheese blend, and
cheese that is packaged already grated, shredded, cubed or sliced.

Wisconsin Milk Marketing Board, the organization that represents the state's dairy farm families, is proud
to sponsor this collection of fine recipes from Wisconsin restaurants. We invite you to enjoy the fine
cheese and dairy products from America's Dairyland, and *Our Best Cookbook 2*.

OUR BEST COOKBOOK 2
CONTRIBUTING RESTAURANTS AND THEIR RECIPES

GUIDE TO CONTRIBUTING MEMBERS' RESTAURANTS

Abrams—Hi-Way Restaurant

Antigo—Leffel's Supper Club

Cambridge—Cambridge Country Inn and Pub

Campbellsport—The Amber Hotel

Cornucopia—The Village Inn

Delavan—Millie's Restaurants

Eagle River—Chinnock's of the North

Fish Creek—The Cookery Restaurant

Green Bay—Rock Garden Supper Club

Green Lake—The Goose Blind, etc.

Hudson—Garfield's Valley House

Kohler—The Wisconsin Room of The American Club

Lake Delton—Annie's Port; The Del-Bar

Lake Geneva—The Grandview Restaurant and Lounge; Ristorante Brissago

Madison—The Bistro at the Madison Concourse Hotel; Irish Waters;
Kavanaughs' Esquire Club; The Kennedy Manor Dining Room & Bar;
Old Town Pub; The Wilson Street Grill

Manitowish Waters—The Blue Bayou Inn Restaurant; The Pine Baron's

Marshfield—Belvedere Supper Club

Merrimac—The Cornucopia Room at Devil's Head Resort;
The Oaks Dining & Spirits; The Sandhill Inn

Milwaukee—333–An American Restaurant; Au Bon Appetit Restaurant;
Grenadier's Restaurant, Inc.; Karl Ratzsch's Restaurant; The Pfister Hotel;
Third Street Pier

Minocqua—Polecat & Lace

Mountain—Tailgate Restaurant & Motel

New Glarus—New Glarus Hotel

Oconto—The Brothers Three; Wayne's Family Restaurant

Osseo—The Norske Nook

Portage—Blankenhaus—The Haus of Good Food

Sauk City—Vern's Dorf Haus

Sister Bay—The Inn at Kristofer's

Stevens Point—Bernard's Country Inn

Superior—Belknap South Restaurant & Lounge

Tomah—Burnstad's European Cafe

Van Dyne—Wendt's on the Lake

Waunakee—The O'Malley Farm Cafe

Wausau—2510 Restaurant; Gulliver's Landing Waterfront Restaurant

Wauwatosa—Chancery Pub & Restaurant

Williams Bay—George Williams College Educational Centers

Wisconsin Dells—American Club & Polish-American Buffet

Map   21

On behalf of the Wisconsin Restaurant Association Education Foundation, thank you for purchasing a copy of *Our Best Cookbook 2*. The proceeds of this cookbook go to administer and distribute scholarships to worthy individuals who are studying to enter the wonderful and rewarding field of the foodservice industry.

This recipe was developed by me, the former "Chef Jeff," while working in the industry as an executive chef. This recipe exemplified to my customers a down-home, hearty, good ol' Wisconsin-style chowder made with fresh, local ingredients. It became one of my signature soups. With a little ingenuity, you can produce a very similar heart-healthy version that will taste almost as good but without the guilt.

I hope you enjoy it!

Jeffrey S. Igel
Senior Director
WRA Education Foundation

WISCONSIN CHICKEN AND SWEET CORN CHOWDER

1	cup medium-diced bacon
3/4	cup medium-diced yellow onion
1/3	cup Wisconsin butter
1/3	cup flour
4	cups chicken stock
2	cups peeled, medium-diced red potatoes
3/4	cup medium-diced green pepper
3/4	cup medium-diced red pepper
2	cups sweet whole kernel corn
2	cups skinless, boneless, cooked chicken
	White pepper to taste
	Seasoning salt to taste
1	cup half-and-half

In soup pot, fry bacon, onions, and butter until bacon is almost crispy. Add flour to make a seasoned roux. Add chicken stock and stir. Add potatoes, peppers, corn, chicken, white pepper, and salt. Bring to a boil and quickly reduce to a simmer. Allow to simmer for 30 minutes. Finish with half-and-half.

Serve and enjoy!

Yields 8 servings

I created this recipe when I discovered some fresh morels I'd purchased were a little mature, so I decided to immediately use them by making something up that my wife and I could enjoy on the deck with a bottle of champagne. Since then, we have enjoyed this recipe with many friends on special occasions.

Ed Lump
Executive Vice President
Wisconsin Restaurant Association

Ed has an extensive background in the restaurant industry as an owner, manager and consultant. He has recently been awarded the prestigious Food Management Professional (FMP) certification from the Educational Foundation of the National Restaurant Association.

ED LUMP'S WILD MUSHROOM APPETIZER

This is a simple but elegant recipe, and like most recipes, proves that food is fun and necessity is the mother of invention.

6	ounces wild mushrooms
	(morels or portobellos are best)
2	tablespoons salt-free Wisconsin butter
1/4	cup Madeira wine
1	cube chicken bouillon
1/2	cup warm water
1	teaspoon cornstarch
2	ounces Wisconsin Blue cheese, crumbled

Chop mushrooms into 1/2-inch pieces. Saute in butter until butter is completely absorbed and mushrooms are brown. Add Madeira wine and saute until caramelized.

Dissolve bouillon cube in warm water and dissolve cornstarch in bouillon mixture; add to mushrooms. Add cheese and stir until combined and thickened.

Serve with high quality crackers.

Yields 2-4 servings

THREE·THIRTY·THREE
AN·AMERICAN
RESTAURANT

333–An American Restaurant
333 West Kilbourn Avenue
Milwaukee, Wisconsin 53203
414-276-1234

Open Thursday and Friday
5:00 p.m. to 9:00 p.m.

Saturday 5:00 p.m. to 9:30 p.m.

All major credit cards accepted

333-An American Restaurant overlooks the majestic atrium of the Hyatt Regency Milwaukee hotel. Our downtown location offers convenient access to the theater, symphony, ballet, and other downtown events.

Enjoy the quiet, intimate setting—perfect for a romantic night out. Our menu is a diverse collection of American cuisine featuring selections from around the country. Washington State Salmon, Texas T-bone Steak and Wisconsin Roast Duckling are just a few of our many selections.

Adjoining the restaurant is the Crystal Room with two walls of colorful cut glass. This beautiful room is ideal for small, private parties or dinner meetings.

Let our experienced staff pamper you with superb service while you enjoy some of Chef Mario Chiappetti's creations at 333-An American Restaurant.

CHAMPAGNE POACHED COHO SALMON WITH SAFFRON CREAM SAUCE

This special entree is perfect when you want to impress your guests.
If you do the preparation of chopping and cleaning the spices and frying the
leeks early in the day or the day before, then the cooking is quick and easy.

2 cups dry champagne	Saffron Cream Sauce:
2 shallots, halved	1 tablespoon Wisconsin butter, clarified
2 cloves fresh garlic	2 shallots, quartered
2 stems fresh dill, chopped	2 cloves fresh garlic, halved
3 large leaves fresh basil, chopped	1 teaspoon salt
2 stems fresh thyme, chopped	Pinch of white pepper
1 teaspoon fresh oregano, chopped	Pinch of saffron
Pinch of salt	1/2 cup white wine
Pinch of white pepper	4 cups Wisconsin heavy cream
4 7 1/2-ounce Coho salmon filets, skinned and deboned	

Vegetable:
2   cups fresh leeks, washed,
        segmented, julienned, dried
    Oil for fryer

Garnish:
4   tablespoons Wisconsin butter, clarified
1/2   cup yellow onion, julienned
1/2   cup shiitake mushroom, julienned
1   cup spinach, cleaned
    Salt and pepper to taste

In large skillet, combine champagne, shallots, garlic, dill, basil, thyme, oregano, salt and pepper. Bring mixture to a simmer over low heat. Add Coho salmon and cover. When salmon is done to your taste, remove from heat and leave covered to keep warm.

To make sauce, combine butter, shallots, garlic, salt, pepper, and saffron in a medium heavy-bottomed saucepan and simmer over low heat. Add white wine and reduce by one-half. Add heavy cream and reduce by one-half or to desired consistency. Stir constantly while cooking and watch sauce to prevent burning.

To prepare vegetables, set deep fryer to 350 degrees. Fry small batches of leeks until golden-crisp. Place on plate with paper towel to drain oil.

For garnish, heat butter in saute pan over medium heat. Add onions and mushrooms, sauteing until onions are golden. Add spinach and season to taste with salt and pepper. Keep warm.

To serve, place 3/4 of garnish in center of plate. Place Coho salmon on garnish. Be careful when handling the fish; it is delicate. Top salmon with remainder of garnish. Ladle sauce around salmon. Lean fried leeks to one side of salmon. Bon Appetite!

Yields 4 servings

2510 Restaurant
2510 Stewart Avenue
Wausau, Wisconsin 54401
715-845-2510

Open daily 11:00 a.m. to 10:00 p.m.

All major credit cards accepted

The 2510 Restaurant and Deli/Bakery is an evolution of over 20 years of restaurant ownership by Pat and Sue Baumer in the greater Wausau area. Their concept of food and hospitality has taken this restaurant to a ranking of 248th in the Restaurant Hospitality's Top 500 Independent Restaurants in the country.

2510 prides itself on the ability to satisfy all diners. Freshly made bread, soups, and an array of salads prepared daily in the deli/bakery complement a vast lunch and dinner menu, offering selections from burgers to lobster and steaks cut daily.

The guests of 2510 have witnessed many renovations over the years. The original restaurant was only one-third the size of the present operation. Currently we are finishing our fourth expansion which has added to our deli/bakery and also provided us with a private dining room.

All of the growth and change has been a tremendous challenge to the management and staff—challenges that have been met with enthusiasm and excitement. In May of 1993, the restaurant went entirely smoke-free. This was done primarily to protect our staff and guests from the harmful effects of second-hand smoke. 2510 thrives on being on the cutting edge of the hospitality industry and will always reach out to this ever-changing market!

2510's STIR-FRY

Seafood, sirloin or chicken is a delightful alternative to give
variety to this already tasty dish.

3/4	cup chopped fresh broccoli
3/4	cup chopped fresh zucchini
1/2	cup chopped fresh carrots
1/2	cup chopped fresh celery
1/4	cup chopped fresh onion
1/2	cup fresh sugar snap peas
1	5-ounce can water chestnuts
1/2	cup fresh red pepper, cut into spears
1/2	cups sliced fresh mushrooms
4	tablespoons Wisconsin butter

Stir-Fry Sauce:

1/2	cup sugar
1/2	cup ketchup
1/3	cup soy sauce
1/3	cup vinegar
2	tablespoons cornstarch
1/4	cup pineapple juice

Combine all vegetables in 4-quart mixing bowl and set aside.

Mix all sauce ingredients in 4-cup measuring cup or small bowl and set aside.

Set burner on medium-high heat. Melt butter in large saute pan. Add mixed vegetables; stir to coat. Cover and allow to steam approximately 10 minutes; stir occasionally. Add sauce and stir to coat all vegetables. Heat until sauce boils; sauce will thicken as it heats.

Serve over hot cooked rice or pasta.

Yields 4-6 servings

The Amber Hotel
139 West Main Street
PO Box 407
Campbellsport, Wisconsin 53010
414-533-8816

Open for lunch Monday and Wednesday through Friday
11:00 a.m. to 2:00 p.m.

Dinner Monday and Wednesday through Saturday
from 4:00 p.m.

Sunday 11:30 a.m. to 8:00 p.m.

MasterCard and Visa accepted

The Amber Hotel has a rich and interesting history. It was known as Bauer's many years ago and it was also known to have the largest hotel and tavern keeper on record, namely Ed "Mush" Bauer. "Mush" is now fondly remembered as our friendly ghost. Our establishment was built in the 1870s and was always a welcoming stop. We try to continue this tradition today as well. Our customers enjoy the relaxed atmosphere and have often mentioned they feel like they are sitting in their own living room.

Travelers touring the Kettle Moraine State Forest enjoy stopping in for our homemade soups and muffins. There is a full bar to relax in and a menu complete with steaks, seafood, and sandwiches.

Because the dining room decor changes with the seasons, you will never be bored with the atmosphere at The Amber.

OUR SPECIAL SEAFOOD SALAD

Even though this recipe has quite a few ingredients,
we guarantee a smile on your guests' faces when they eat it.
This salad is especially nice to serve to women,
accompanying it with fresh fruit and muffins.

2	cups frozen salad shrimp, unthawed
2	cups flaked imitation crab
1	cup frozen peas, unthawed
1/2	cup chopped onions
1/2	cup chopped green pepper
1/2	cup chopped celery
1	8-ounce package Wisconsin cream cheese, softened
1	cup Wisconsin sour cream
2	tablespoons lemon juice
1	tablespoon dill weed
1/4	teaspoon white pepper
	Garlic powder, garlic salt, onion powder, onion salt, and celery salt to taste
1	cup catsup
1-2	tablespoons horseradish, or to taste

In a large bowl, toss together the shrimp, crab, peas, onions, green pepper, and celery; set aside. In a separate bowl, mix together remaining ingredients until smooth. Pour over seafood mixture and blend. Chill for several hours before serving.

Yields 6-8 servings

American Club & Polish-American Buffet
(Formerly Dick's Polish-American Smorgasbord)
400 County A & Highway 12
Wisconsin Dells, Wisconsin 53965
608-253-4451

Open daily 3:00 p.m. to 9:00 p.m.

Open Sundays and Holidays 1:00 p.m. to 8:00 p.m.

All major credit cards accepted

Richard and Grace Makowski emigrated from Poland in 1964 and began their business lives in Wisconsin Dells in 1971. They presently are owners of American World, which consists of American Club & Polish-American Buffet, Inn, Resort, Liquor Store, and Continental Motel. Their four children are active in the operation of the business.

Guests enjoy the all-you-can-eat buffet featuring such delicacies as pierogi (dumplings), golabki (stuffed cabbage), U.S. choice roast beef, roast or fried chicken, snitzels and much more.

POTATO PANCAKES (PLACKI KARTOFLANE)

*This potato pancake recipe is a customer favorite
brought here from Poland by Grace Makowski of the
American Club & Polish-American Buffet.*

5	large potatoes, grated
2	large onions, grated
3	eggs, beaten
2	cups flour
1	tablespoon salt
1	teaspoon pepper
	Shortening for frying

Mix potatoes, onions, eggs, flour, salt and pepper thoroughly. Heat shortening in heavy skillet. Drop batter by spoonfuls onto skillet. Flatten each pancake with a fork; fry until first side is golden brown. Turn pancakes and fry until second side is browned.

Yields 20-25 medium-sized pancakes

Annie's Port
51675 Ishnala Road
PO Box 449
Lake Delton, Wisconsin 53940
608-254-8230

Open daily Memorial Day to Labor Day at 4:00 p.m.

American Express, MasterCard, and Visa accepted

Annie's Port is a little treasure amid the pines on Mirror Lake. The dining room seats about 50 casual diners. Since 1965 guests, both locals and tourists, have been treated to famous pizza and pasta, plus salads, sandwiches and cocktails. Our pizza sauce recipe is a family secret and is used in many of our Italian dishes.

RAINBOW CHEESECAKE

The "crust" for this cheesecake cuts down on prep time and has much less sugar and fat than a more traditional crust. The fat in the cake itself is lessened with the reduction of egg yolks. When making this at home, you may use part low-fat cream cheese and try it with peach or melon slices instead of orange.

"Crust":
- 2 teaspoons Wisconsin butter
- 7 graham cracker squares or about 2 ounces vanilla wafer crumbs

Cake:
- 4 8-ounce packages Wisconsin cream cheese, softened
- 1¼ cups sugar
- 5 large egg whites
- 3 large whole eggs
- 1 teaspoon lemon juice
- ½ teaspoon vanilla

Glaze:
- ¾ cup orange juice
- 1 tablespoon cornstarch
- 3 tablespoons sugar
- ⅛ cup lemon juice
- ½ teaspoon grated orange zest
    Dash of nutmeg and mace

Topping:
- 1 pint strawberries, sliced
- 1 11-ounce can mandarin oranges
- 3 slices pineapple (canned or fresh) cut in wedges
- 1 kiwi, peeled, sliced, and slices halved
- 3-5 blueberries or purple grapes

Generously coat bottom and sides of 10-inch springform pan with butter. Sprinkle crumbs over butter and tap and tilt pan to cover evenly.

Beat cream cheese in mixer bowl, gradually to medium speed. Add sugar. Continue beating. Reduce speed and gradually add eggs. Add lemon juice and vanilla. Increase speed and fluff mixture, about 1 minute. Pour into crumb-coated pan. Bake at 225 degrees for 2 hours until cake begins to pull from sides of pan. Turn off oven and leave in another 2 hours. This slow baking process prevents cake from cracking. Loosen spring sides. Remove cake from bottom tin. (A strip of dental floss, held firmly, placed at far edge and pulled under crumb layer helps loosen cake evenly.) With large pancake turner, slide cake to large flat plate. Refrigerate.

To make glaze, mix juice, cornstarch and sugar in small saucepan. Bring to boil, stirring constantly. Boil 1 minute. Remove from heat. Add lemon juice, zest and spices. Cool 20 minutes. Spread evenly over top of cake.

Arrange fruit decoratively over glaze in a spectrum of color: red, orange, yellow, green, blue. Place each fruit in a circle, beginning with strawberries around the outer edge. Use only half the can of oranges, saving remainder for another use. Work toward middle, ending with a flower of kiwi petals and center of blueberries. Refrigerate. Best served within 6 hours after applying glaze and fruit.

Yields 10-12 servings

Au Bon Appetit Restaurant
1016 East Brady Street
Milwaukee, Wisconsin 53202
414-278-1233

Open for lunch Monday through Friday
11:00 a.m. to 3:00 p.m.

Dinner Monday through Thursday 5:00 p.m. to 9:00 p.m.
Friday 5:00 p.m. to 10:00 p.m.
Saturday 11:00 a.m. to 10:00 p.m.

MasterCard and Visa accepted

Au Bon Appetit is a Mediterranean restaurant, with Lebanese cuisine per se. It was established in May 1991 and is owned by chef Rihab Aris, her two sons, Wael and Amer and their partner, Costi Helou.

The restaurant seats about 30 people. The decor is European and the atmosphere is cozy, romantic and known for memorable special occasions. Hot pink and white linen cover the tables. Fresh flowers and candles add a magic touch to the ambience.

The menu emphasizes the vegetarian aspect of the food items. It features a large variety of fresh, healthy and tasty vegetarian choices such as Hummos (Chick Pea Dip), Baba Ghannouj (Eggplant Dip), Falafel (Ground Faua & Garbanzo Bean Fritters), and Tabbouleh Salad (Seasoned Cracked Wheat with Fresh Vegetables). In addition, the menu features some French dishes like Poulet Basquaise and Ratatouille Provencale as well as lean lamb, beef, and chicken specialties and daily specials. Local and imported wine and beer are also served.

Au Bon Appetit has been selected as one of the top 25 restaurants in Milwaukee by Mr. Dennis Getto, Milwaukee Journal food critic and as one of the city's best restaurants by Mr. Willard Romantini, Milwaukee Magazine food critic. Moreover, chef Rihab Aris has been honored as one of North America's outstanding 2,000 chefs in 1993 and 1994.

Au Bon Appetit has been selected as the East Town Association Committee's favorite at Bastille Festival in 1994. Dining at Au Bon Appetit is a memorable experience.

LE DELICE DES VEGETARIENS
"THE VEGETARIANS' DELICACY"

2	large eggplants
1/2	cup olive oil
2	large onions, peeled and sliced
32	black olives, pitted
32	cloves garlic, peeled
4	medium tomatoes, sliced
	Salt to taste

Wash eggplants and partly peel vertically, leaving stripes of black skin to keep them held together firmly while cooking. Remove stems. Cut each eggplant vertically into equal halves. Starting at bottom of eggplant, cut vertical slits or "fingers" up to within a few inches of the top, keeping the upper part attached.

Put oil in shallow pan and place rings of onion on bottom of pan. Place eggplant halves on top of onion rings. In between the fingers of the eggplant, place pitted olives, cloves of garlic and sliced tomatoes. Add salt to taste. Cover with aluminum foil and bake in a 400-degree oven for approximately 45 minutes. Serve with cooked rice, bread, and salad.

Yields 4 servings

THE BELKNAP SOUTH RESTAURANT

· FINE FAMILY DINING · AT THE AIRPORT

Belknap South Restaurant & Lounge
1415 North 46th Street
Superior, Wisconsin 54880
715-394-3313

*Serving Tuesday through Friday
11:00 a.m. to 9:00 p.m.
Saturday 8:00 a.m. to 9:00 p.m.
Sunday 8:00 a.m. to 8:00 p.m.*

MasterCard and Visa accepted

It all started as an airport hangar with a small cafe upstairs. The hangar/cafe combination soon established a reputation as a convenient place for small aircraft commuters to stop and refuel their airplanes and grab a quick bite to eat.

By 1980, with the success of the cafe demanding more room, a full service restaurant and lounge was built in the space where the airplane hangar was located. The establishment was renamed the Belknap South, taking its name from the owner's previous restaurant, which was located just a few miles north on Belknap Street.

Today, the South's distinction as a quality dining and entertainment experience has made it a favorite with everyone from families to pilots and skydivers.

CHARLIE'S CORNISH GAME HENS A LA APPLE SAUCE

This recipe is excellent with pheasant and grouse also.

4	Cornish game hens
3/4	cup flour
2	tablespoons Wisconsin butter
1	large onion
3	large apples
	Wisconsin whole milk
	White pepper and basil to taste

Lightly flour game hens. Heat butter in large roasting pan on stove top. Place hens in pan and brown on all sides. Arrange hens breast side up.

Slice large onion in 1/4-inch rings and place them over top of birds. Peel and core 3 large apples; cut into 1-inch pieces and place chunks around birds. Pour whole milk 1/2 way up the birds. Sprinkle lightly with white pepper and basil. Cover and roast 1 hour at 325 degrees. Serve hens with onion apple sauce.

Yields 4 servings

Belvedere Supper Club
M329 Highway 97
Marshfield, Wisconsin 54449
715-387-4161

Open daily 4:00 p.m.

Monday through Friday 11:00 a.m. to 2:00 p.m.

Sunday Brunch 10:00 a.m. to 2:00 p.m.

All major credit cards accepted

The Belvedere Supper Club is located on Highway 97, just three miles north of Marshfield, and six miles south of Stratford.

Restaurants are nothing new to the owners of The Belvedere, whose name, Leffel, means "spoon" in German. Dale Leffel's great uncle, Fred Klumb, started his restaurant in 1934 in Marquette, Michigan. With Fred as their mentor, the Leffel's carry on the traditions of fine food and good service in a pleasant clean surrounding with a natural wood decor. Built in 1984, the 50th anniversary of Fred's beginning, The Belvedere upholds the same friendly style that Dale's great uncle established over the years.

Set in a pleasant country atmosphere, The Belvedere Supper Club offers several dining room options. Upon entering The Belvedere, you are greeted by the Oak Lounge Bar. The Portico Room offers a large banquet reception hall with its own private bar. For a smaller private non-smoking dining area, there is the Fireside Room. All dining areas are complemented by The Belvedere's friendly staff.

Lovely weddings can also be held at an outdoor chapel located on the beautiful grounds.

ROAST DUCK LEFFEL

3	ducks
	Ginger
	Seasoning salt
	Pepper
¹/₂	pound pork sausage
1	cup diced onions
¹/₂	pound fresh mushrooms, sliced
16	cups bread crumbs
¹/₂	tablespoon sage
2	cups beef stock, more if necessary

Apple Brandy Glaze:

1	cup sugar
1	cup water
1	cup apple juice
¹/₂	cup raisins
1	shot brandy

Place ducks on grated tray to keep them above their drippings. Sprinkle lightly with ginger, seasoning salt, and pepper.

To make stuffing, simmer pork sausage, onions, and sliced mushrooms on low heat until golden brown. Then add bread crumbs, sage and beef stock, adding more beef stock if necessary for a moist dressing. For fullest flavor, stuff duck cavity before baking.

Bake ducks at 375 degrees until tender, 4-6 hours. After cooled slightly, use the flat side of a cleaver to break down the breastbone. Then split duck in half.

To make Apple Brandy Glaze, boil sugar, water, and apple juice in medium saucepan until liquid has a syrup-like texture. Then add raisins. Heat juice mixture and raisins. Remove pan from heat and add brandy (or add at tableside). Allow brandy to burn off then pour glaze over duck halves.

Servings 6

Bernard's Country Inn
701 Second Street North
Stevens Point, Wisconsin 54481
715-344-3365

Open daily from 4:00 p.m.

All major credit cards accepted

Since 1973, Bernard Kurzawa has been known in central Wisconsin for his European and American specials. Bernard is a European-trained Master Chef who has received many awards and was named 1994 Restaurateur of the Year by the Wisconsin Restaurant Association. Bernard makes everything on the premises from soup and pickles to classic continental pastries and desserts.

Bernard's has a casual atmosphere and elegant service.

PORK WISCONSIN STYLE

This low calorie dish has great presentation. Serve with baby carrots and small Wisconsin red potatoes or vegetables of your choice.

---

3   pounds boneless pork loin
1   large greening apple
1/4   cup white wine
1/4   cup flour
6   tablespoons Wisconsin butter
1/2   cup red wine
1/2   cup brown sauce (sauce Espagnol)
    Salt and pepper to taste

Cranberry Sauce:
1   12-ounce bag cranberries
1/2   cup water
    Grated rind of 1/2 lemon
1   pinch ground cinnamon
3/4   cup sugar

Trim pork loin of all fats and silverskins. Cut into 6 steaks, butterfly and pound to 1/4-inch thick; set aside. Peel and core apple and cut into 1/4-inch slices. Steam in small saucepan with white wine until tender; do not overcook. Set aside.

To make cranberry sauce, put cranberries into small saucepan. Add water, lemon rind and cinnamon. Cover and simmer on low heat for 10 minutes. Stir in sugar and pass sauce through fine sieve to remove seeds and skins. Set aside.

Heat butter in large skillet. Flour pork steaks and saute at low temperature. Do not overcook! Remove steaks and arrange on platter. Deglaze skillet with red wine. Add brown sauce and cranberry sauce; simmer. Add salt and pepper to taste, pour sauce over pork steaks, and garnish with apple slices.

Yields 6 servings

T H E B I S T R O

The Bistro at the Madison Concourse Hotel
1 West Dayton Street
Madison, Wisconsin 53704
608-257-6000

Open daily 5:00 p.m. to 10:00 p.m.

All major credit cards accepted

The Bistro has been highly acclaimed as one of the area's finest restaurants. The Bistro menu features fine continental cuisine and offers a diverse selection of appetizers, entrees, vegetarian specialties, as well as fine wines and exquisite desserts. Your choices range from Chef Brian's fresh catch of the day, certified Angus beef, grilled barbecue shrimp, pasta specialties, and much more.

For an intimate dinner for two or to entertain friends and family, let The Bistro at the Madison Concourse Hotel be your choice for a fine dining experience.

Also join us in the Dayton Street Cafe & Bakery serving breakfast, lunch, and featuring our 20-foot salad bar or our award-winning Sunday brunch served 9:30 a.m. to 1:30 p.m.

WISCONSIN CHICKEN CORDON BLEU

This Chicken Cordon Bleu is a "fun with food" version. It stands apart from the norm because of the use of a variety of quality ingredients that can be found locally. We hope you'll enjoy this recipe as much as we have, and if for some reason you would like to change something to meet your individual desires, please do so. After all, we all like to have "fun with food."

½	bulb fresh garlic (approximately 6 large cloves)
4	tablespoons olive oil, divided
4	ounces Wisconsin Gorgonzola cheese
6	ounces Wisconsin Chevre, crumbled
4	6-ounce chicken breasts (with or without skin)
4	ounces proscuitto (dry-cured spiced ham)
3	tablespoons all-purpose flour

Door County Cherry Sauce:

⅓	cup pitted Door County cherries
¼	cup red currant jelly
¼	cup Port wine or grape juice
1	tablespoon water
1	tablespoon cornstarch

In small covered baking dish, roast peeled garlic cloves in 2 tablespoons olive oil for 30 minutes at 350 degrees. Set aside to cool. After garlic has cooled, smash it with the edge of a knife until a paste forms.

In small mixing bowl, blend both cheeses and garlic paste until well mixed. Lay each chicken breast on flat surface and gently pound with meat tenderizer to make chicken even for filling and cooking. Place ¼ of proscuitto in center of each breast and top with ¼ of cheese mixture.

Roll breast and place toothpicks on 2 sides to hold together. Lightly roll chicken in flour to coat. Using skillet, sear chicken in 2 tablespoons olive oil over medium-high heat just until lightly browned. Remove chicken from skillet and place in shallow baking pan. Bake in preheated 350-degree oven for 30 minutes.

To make sauce, bring cherries, jelly, and Port wine to boil in small saucepan. Mix water and cornstarch, adding to boiling mixture to thicken. Serve over chicken breasts.

Yields 4 servings

Blankenhaus—The Haus of Good Food
1223 East Wisconsin
Portage, Wisconsin 53901
608-742-7555

Open for lunch Tuesday through Friday
11:00 a.m. to 2:00 p.m.

Dinner Tuesday through Thursday
4:30 p.m. to 10:00 p.m.
Friday and Saturday 4:30 p.m. to 11:00 p.m.
Sunday 2:00 p.m. to 10:00 p.m.

Sunday brunch 11:00 a.m. to 2:00 p.m.

MasterCard and Visa accepted

A Portage landmark known in years past as "The Roost," the restaurant was acquired by the Blankenheim family in 1978. Extensive remodeling to the building followed and was reopened in 1979 as The Blankenhaus. This name was taken from the German name "Blankenheim" which means clean or white home.

Today this popular dining spot is operated by Jim and Kay Blankenheim who took over the well-known restaurant in 1985 from Jim's parents, Romie and Pauline Blankenheim. Over a period of 40 years, Romie and Pauline had owned and operated several successful restaurants in Portage and other Wisconsin cities, with a reputation for efficient service and fine food at reasonable prices.

Jim, Kay, and the entire staff constantly work to improve and fine tune the business to meet the ever-changing tastes of their customers who come from far and wide to enjoy the ambiance and tasty cuisine.

Thanks to past and present employees and our wonderful and loyal customers, the restaurant has been the recipient of several awards over the years. The Blankenhaus is dedicated to paying close attention to detail, food and service in a thoroughly friendly and comfortable atmosphere so that it will remain one of the favorite gathering places in the area.

BLANKENHAUS ELEGANT BAKED COD

*Even though it's easy to prepare, you'll get compliments galore on this
elegant entree. You may vary it by tucking fresh, sliced, buttered
mushrooms around the fish before baking. Or mashed potatoes
could be piped around the outside or accompany the cod
with cooked broccoli flowers or asparagus spears. Try it!
We created it in our kitchen and were delighted with the results.*

8	tablespoons Wisconsin butter, melted
3	pounds cod, thawed
1	cup ranch dressing
1	cup crushed Italian seasoned croutons
	Paprika
	Lemon wedges and parsley, garnish

Put 1 tablespoon butter into 8 individual casseroles or ramekins. Cut fish into 6-ounce portions and place one in each casserole. Put 2 tablespoons of ranch dressing on each piece of fish. Top with 2 tablespoons crouton crumbs and sprinkle with paprika. Bake uncovered at 350 degrees for 30-45 minutes. Fish is done when it flakes and is no longer translucent.

Serve with lemon wedge and parsley.

Yields 8 servings

The Blue Bayou Inn Restaurant
US Highway 51
Manitowish Waters, Wisconsin 54545
715-543-2537 or 1-800-533-9671

*Open Monday through Saturday,
late April through October,
serving from 5:00 p.m.*

Discover, MasterCard and Visa accepted

The Blue Bayou Inn—a restaurant that has truly set itself apart from the others in the Northwoods! Through the efforts of Chef Walt Mazur, his wife Rita, his family, and a fine staff, The Blue Bayou Inn has become one of the finest restaurants in the Northwoods, if not in the entire state of Wisconsin.

Chef Walter trained in the kitchens of Louisiana and brought that state's cookery to Wisconsin via the Northwoods of Manitowish Waters. Real Louisiana food is a symphony of flavor that requires a maestro's hand in seasoning and preparation. Only a few restaurants have taken Louisiana cooking seriously, and The Blue Bayou is one. The menu features specialties learned from Louisiana chefs—Crawfish or Shrimp Etouffee, Bayou Kitchen Jambalaya, and catfish served six different ways, to name just a few.

In addition to Louisiana cuisine, The Blue Bayou's extensive menu includes all-American fare as well. A favorite of many is the Angler's Special: "Bring in the fish you caught today and we'll prepare it just the way you like," promises our chef. You'll also find an excellent selection of appetizers, soups and salads. One shouldn't overlook the authentic southern desserts that will tantalize any sweet-tooth. If you enjoy a cocktail, you'll find your favorite in the Steamboat Lounge.

The Blue Bayou has distinguished itself as something of a dining legend by way of its authentic cuisine and captivating atmosphere and has received accolades from various publications including a 4-star rating from the Milwaukee Journal in 1988.

Chef Wally Mazur died March 18, 1994 from cancer. Because of his vast knowledge and love of the restaurant business that he so openly and willingly shared, his wife Rita, his family and staff are able to carry on the fine tradition of The Blue Bayou Inn that was started 15 years ago by the one and only "Chef Walter."

CRAWFISH ETOUFFEE-SPICY

*This recipe was one of Chef Walter's favorites to teach in his
"Louisiana School of Cooking in Wisconsin" class.
He felt the preparation as well as the cooking time was quick and easy
for the most impromptu dinner party. By using whole wheat products
and brown rice, he felt it was healthful as well as flavorful!*

6	cups finely chopped onions
3	cups finely chopped green peppers
1½	cups finely chopped celery
2	tablespoons finely chopped parsley
1	tablespoon sweet basil
1	tablespoon Worcestershire sauce
1	tablespoon hot sauce
1	tablespoon sea salt
1	teaspoon cayenne pepper
½	teaspoon white pepper
½	teaspoon crushed red pepper
½	cup Wisconsin butter
2	cups water
3	tablespoons tomato paste
2	tablespoons flour, whole wheat preferred
1	pound crawfish tail meat, cooked and peeled
4	cups cooked rice, natural brown preferred

Place vegetables, herbs, spices and butter into large saucepan. Cook over medium heat until soft and actually sticking to the bottom of the pot, 15-20 minutes. Gently scrape the bottom of the pot, freeing up all the ingredients that may be stuck. Add water for the purpose of deglazing and cook for 2-3 minutes. Add tomato paste, flour, and crawfish tails and simmer until thickened, 10-15 minutes. Taste for salt content and serve over rice.

Sprinkle with parsley and serve with French bread and your favorite chardonnay.

Yields 6-8 servings

The Brothers Three
106 Superior Avenue
Oconto, Wisconsin 54153
414-834-3471

Open daily 11:00 a.m. to 12:00 p.m.

MasterCard and Visa accepted

The Brothers Three, located on the Oconto River in Oconto, is a full-service restaurant, specializing in pizzas made from scratch, Mexican entrees, and fine cocktails. Our cocktail lounge offers a scenic view of the river, with boat docking available. An outside deck provides dining enjoyment during the summer months. Wisconsin lottery tickets are sold here.

Our dining room features a newly-decorated private room, perfect for your banquets, private meetings, showers, or other occasions. We take pride in the variety of services we offer, such as birthday parties for pre-schoolers to pre-teens, excellent luncheon service, and senior citizen discounts.

We suggest our daily soup-and-sandwich special on our home-baked breads and rolls for your noon-hour enjoyment. Please the family with our large pizzas-and-pitcher of soda special on Thursdays or with our mouth-watering fish frys on Fridays. Enjoy casual dining at its best on Saturday nights with your choice of a delicious stir-fry or a chicken dinner with all of the trimmings on Sundays. We offer noon-hour delivery service to your home or place of business and full delivery service after 4:30 p.m. daily. We are ready to handle any request to cater to your company meeting or employee picnic. Banquet and catering menus are available on request. We pride ourselves on offering the best in food and courteous service.

SEAFOOD NACHOS

*This recipes was created at The Brothers Three
and has been voted a favorite by our customers. Enjoy!*

3	tortilla shells
	Seasoning salt
1¹/₂	tablespoons chopped onion
1¹/₂	tablespoons chopped green pepper
4	ounces crabmeat, flaked
¹/₂	cup Wisconsin Cheddar cheese sauce, either canned or homemade
¹/₄	tomato, chopped

Cut each tortilla shell into 8 triangles. In large sauce pot, heat ¹/₂ inch oil to hot (or if using a deep-fryer, follow manufacturer's instructions). Fry triangles, a few at a time, for about 30 seconds then turn and fry other side just a few seconds more, until golden brown. Drain on paper towels and sprinkle to taste with seasoning salt; set aside.

Combine onions, green peppers, crabmeat, and cheese sauce and heat in microwave for 30 seconds. Place nachos on small plate. Top with heated mixture and top with tomatoes.

Yields 1 serving

Burnstad's European Cafe
701 East Clifton Street
Tomah, Wisconsin 54660
608-372-4040

Open Sunday 8:00 a.m. to 8:00 p.m.
Monday through Saturday 8:00 a.m. to 9:00 p.m.

All major credit cards accepted

The elegant yet relaxed atmosphere of the European Cafe offers eating at its finest seven days a week—breakfast, lunch and dinner. When we opened for business in August of 1979, we were called the "Garden Cafe" and consisted of a small one-room dining area within what was then called Burnstad's Village Mall. The menu was typewritten on a sheet of paper and cooking took place on a stove borrowed from another employee. The restaurant, with its hardwood floors, butcher-block tables and cane-back chairs, offered a whole new dining concept in our area, which was accustomed to family-style restaurants, drive-ins, and truck stops.

Business grew very rapidly, and plans to expand the restaurant's size, menu, and hours of operation became necessary. About six years ago the Burnstad complex was remodeled and renamed "Burnstad's European Village." Within the Village, an additional dining room was added to the cafe, expanding its seating capacity from 56 to 170. With these changes came menu adaptations which included foods with an international flair like European-style breads, sandwiches, salads, and cuisine along with an elaborate homemade dessert ensemble.

The popularity of the restaurant continues to grow as word of mouth and billboards across the state bring diners from all over the country. Burnstad's prides itself on providing friendly and efficient service while meeting the needs of our customers. The cafe offers take-out meals and encourages "faxed" lunch orders for our local business people who like their meal waiting for them when they arrive.

Due to popular demand, our European-style breads are now offered for sale. Wines and spirits are available any time of the day. We accommodate tour bus groups almost daily.

After having been in business for 15 years, we have been described as "The best kept secret in Wisconsin" and "Door County under one roof."

CARAMELIZED PECAN PIE

This recipe was created by Đea Thornton, the cafe's manager, who,
at that time, was in charge of baking desserts. It is the European Cafe's
most requested recipe. It has been published in the La Crosse Tribune
and the Milwaukee Journal. We have received many wonderful comments
about the recipe with our favorite being "died and went to heaven."

1	15-ounce bag caramels, unwrapped
1/2	cup Wisconsin butter
1	6-ounce can evaporated milk
1	cup chopped pecans
1	10-inch unbaked pie crust
2	8-ounce packages Wisconsin cream cheese
1/2	cup sugar
2	eggs
1	teaspoon vanilla

In small saucepan, melt together caramels, butter, and evaporated milk. Stir until smooth. Place pecans in bottom of unbaked pie crust. Lightly spread all but 1 cup of caramel mixture over pecans. Reserve remaining caramel mixture.

Soften cream cheese with mixer until fluffy. Add sugar, eggs, and vanilla and pour batter over caramel layer. Bake at 350 degrees until pie is set in center, about 35 to 40 minutes. Set aside to cool.

Top with reserved caramel mixture and garnish with a sprinkle of pecans in the middle of the pie.

Yields 8-10 servings

cambridge country
INN & PUB

Cambridge Country Inn and Pub
206 West Main Street
Cambridge, Wisconsin 53523
608-423-3275

Open Sunday through Thursday
7:00 a.m. to 9:00 p.m.

Friday and Saturday 7:00 a.m. to 10:00 p.m.

MasterCard and Visa accepted

There's nothing more satisfying than discovering a great home-cooked meal in a pleasant country town, where fresh baked favorites are complemented by a comfortable and charming atmosphere.

If the town is Cambridge, and the restaurant is The Cambridge Country Inn and Pub, you're in for a treat. Nestled about 20 minutes southeast of Madison, near Rowe Pottery Works, the Country Inn and Pub is just far enough off the beaten path for you to take a mental vacation without having to pack anything but your appetite.

Owners Gary and Susan Hammond bought the restaurant over eight years ago and have created a landmark where everyone feels at home. Guests are often lured off Main Street and into the Inn and Pub by the sweet smell of fresh baked goods. Whether you are coming in for coffee and pie, entertaining business guests or getting together with friends for dinner, there's a place for you to feel comfortable.

CHICKEN POT PIE IN PUFF PASTRY

*There's nothing more satisfying than a great home-cooked meal.
Chicken Pot Pie in Puff Pastry is one such offering sure to
delight family and friends.*

Chicken Velote:
- 8 cups chicken stock
- 1/2 teaspoon white pepper
- 1/2 teaspoon black pepper, freshly ground
- 2/3 cup cornstarch (Clear Jel brand works best)

Filling:
- 3 cups sliced carrot, 1/4-inch thick
- 3 cups diced celery, 1/4-inch
- 2 cups green peas, fresh or frozen
- 2 cups whole kernel corn, fresh or frozen
- 3 cups cooked and diced chicken meat, 1/2-inch dice
- 1 teaspoon black pepper, freshly ground
- 1/2 teaspoon salt
- 8 pieces puff pastry squares, 4 x 4-inch*
- 8 pieces leaf lettuce
- 24 pieces assorted fresh fruit

Combine chicken stock and white and black pepper in 4-quart saucepan. Bring to boil; add moistened cornstarch and stir until well mixed. Set aside.

Blanch carrots, celery, peas, and corn; drain. Combine vegetables, cooked chicken meat, black pepper, salt, and reserved velote. Bring to boil. Reduce heat and simmer 15 minutes, stirring constantly. Set aside.

Prepare and bake puff pastry squares according to package directions.

To serve, hollow out center of baked puff pastry square. Place 2 cups filling in each square. Place square on leaf lettuce bed and garnish with fresh fruit.

*Available in most grocery stores

Yields 8 servings

Chancery Pub & Restaurant
7613 West State Street
Wauwatosa, Wisconsin 53213
414-771-3100

*Open Sunday through Thursday
11:00 a.m. to 12:00 p.m.*

Friday and Saturday 11:00 a.m. to 1:00 a.m.

All major credit cards accepted

Few visitors to southeastern Wisconsin can resist the temptation to stop at the Chancery restaurants. Since our beginning in 1972, and now with seven locations, in Racine (2), Milwaukee (2), Wauwatosa, Waukesha, and Mequon, guests can enjoy an eclectic menu in a casual atmosphere. Cheer on your home team in our pubs and enjoy our all-you-can-eat Chicken Feast on Sundays and Tuesdays; all-you-can-eat Shrimp Boil on Mondays; and our famous Long Island Ice Tea Club happening on Tuesdays. The Chancery—where kids are king—also has an extensive children's menu and kid meal program.

There's something for everyone on our huge menu: a wonderful array of appetizers, pasta dishes, seafood selections, crisp delicious salads, and our famous pub burgers. Save room for dessert, as our mouth-watering temptations await you!

The Chancery—One Restaurant, Seven Great Locations! Stop in today!

ARTICHOKE DIP

*At the restaurants, this appetizer, a Chancery original,
is served on boule bread, a loaf infused with cheese and herbs.
Try it too on fresh Italian bread, pita chips or bagel chips.*

2	canned artichoke hearts, drained
1	8-ounce package Wisconsin cream cheese
1	cup grated Wisconsin Parmesan cheese
3/4	cup Wisconsin sour cream
3/4	cup mayonnaise
1	teaspoon garlic powder
1	fresh jalapeno pepper, seeded and finely diced

Preheat oven to 325 degrees. Cut artichoke hearts into quarters and set 6 of the quarters aside. Chop remaining artichoke hearts and mix with all remaining ingredients. Place mixture into 2 medium-sized, fluted baking dishes or 1 9-inch pie pan. Level out mixture in pan and place artichoke quarters symmetrically in center. Bake for 35-40 minutes (longer if using 1 larger baking dish) or until dips are lightly browned on top.

Serve immediately or refrigerate and simply reheat in the microwave when ready to serve.

Yields 4-6 servings

Chinnock's of the North
3385 Highway 70E
Eagle River, Wisconsin 54521
715-479-7757

Open Monday through Saturday 11:00 a.m. to 11:00 p.m.

Diner's Club, Discover, MasterCard and Visa accepted

Located four miles east of Eagle River on State Highway 70, Chinnock's of the North is a down-home, family-style restaurant that didn't forget the family! Specializing in homemade soups, large, juicy hamburgers, famous fish fries and a constant variety of desserts, the menu at Chinnock's is sure to please everyone. The prices are sure to please also!

Enjoy a cocktail or cup of coffee with your dinner as you relax in the friendly, warm atmosphere at Chinnock's. You'll leave full from the ample portions. Best food in the Northwoods—not a brag, just a fact!

Join the friends and family at Chinnock's of the North!

RED, WHITE AND BLUE CHEESECAKE

This low-fat cheesecake is served every Fourth of July at Chinnock's.
The recipe is time-consuming but not difficult and its blend of flavors
and beautiful red, white, and blue layers make it very popular.

1½	cups graham cracker crumbs
6	tablespoons Wisconsin butter, softened
1	cup sugar, divided
1	teaspoon ground ginger
2	¼-ounce envelopes gelatin
¾	cup water
1	16-ounce carton small curd Wisconsin cottage cheese
1	8-ounce package fat-free Wisconsin cream cheese
2	tablespoons lemon juice
1	cup half-and-half
¼	cup blueberry preserves
¼	cup raspberry preserves

Garnishes:
  Small dollop of Wisconsin
     whipped cream
  Sliced strawberries, fresh
  Fresh raspberries
  Fresh blueberries

To prepare crust, blend graham cracker crumbs, butter, ¼ cup sugar, and ginger. Pat into bottom of 10-inch springform pan and refrigerate.

In small saucepan, stir together gelatin, ¾ cup sugar, and water. Bring to boil and boil 1 minute; set aside.

In a food processor, blend cottage cheese, cream cheese, and lemon juice until smooth, about 1 minute. Add half-and-half and blend just until smooth. Add reserved gelatin mixture and combine.

Measure 1⅔ cups mixture and blend blueberry preserves into mix. Pour onto crust and spread evenly; freeze for 10 minutes. Pour 1⅔ cups mixture (white layer) on top of blue layer; freeze for 10 minutes. Blend remaining mixture with raspberry preserves. Pour over white layer. Refrigerate 24 hours. Garnish with whipped cream and fresh berries.

Yields 12-16 servings

The Cookery Restaurant
Highway 42
PO Box 376
Fish Creek, Wisconsin 54212
414-868-3634

Open daily mid-April through October
7:00 a.m. to 9:00 p.m. and winter weekends

Mastercard and Visa accepted

When Dick and Carol Skare embarked on their Door County honeymoon in 1977, they had no idea that they would create a thriving business in the heart of Fish Creek. After 18 years, The Cookery Restaurant remains one of the peninsula's finest eateries.

Serving breakfast, lunch, and dinner, Dick and Carol are always on the lookout for creative new ideas to add to an already fantastic array of menu items. In addition to traditional Door County favorites, the restaurant offers such specialties as The Cookery's famous whitefish chowder (an old family recipe), chicken salad made with cherry chutney, and linguine with garlic pesto sauce. And in response to customer concerns about cholesterol, the Skares worked with a local hospital dietitian to develop authentic Heart Healthy variations of their original recipes.

Most of the homemade delights served in the restaurant are available for purchase in The Pantry Gift Shop located right next door. Opened in 1984, it features The Cookery's vast assortment of items made right on the premises, such as cherry-apple sauce, mustard dill dressing, cherry chutney, apricot mustard sauce, 3-pepper relish and 4-berry jam, all of which can be shipped to family or friends. Specialty food items from around the world are available for purchase as well. The Pantry is also a bakery and deli offering freshly baked breads, pies, and pastries, pasta salads, sandwiches and soup. Cappuccino and espresso may be enjoyed on the patio.

If you should decide to stay, The Cookery provides cottage rentals within walking distance of the beach and spacious apartments with a view of the bay.

The entire staff at The Cookery extends a warm welcome to all of their customers, past and present, and they invite you to visit them soon!

THE COOKERY'S CHUNKY CHICKEN SALAD

The cherry chutney for this signature salad may be ordered from The Cookery's mail order catalog. Or substitute mango chutney for a delicious alternative.

3/4	cup mayonnaise
2	tablespoons cherry chutney
1/2	teaspoon curry powder
1/4	teaspoon salt
1 1/2	cups crushed pineapple, well drained, squeezed dry
1/2	teaspoon lemon juice
2	cups finely chopped, cooked white chicken meat
1	cup diced celery
1/2	cup sliced green onions, cut in small rounds
1/2	tablespoon finely chopped capers

Combine mayonnaise, chutney, curry powder and salt and mix. Add pineapple, lemon juice, chicken, celery, green onions, and capers. Serve plain, over croissants or on multi-grain buns.

Yields 8 servings

DEVIL'S HEAD

Resort & Covention Center

The Cornucopia Room at Devil's Head Resort
S6330 Bluff Road
Merrimac, Wisconsin 53561
608-493-2251

Open Sunday through Thursday 6:00 a.m. to 10:00 p.m.

Friday and Saturday 6:00 a.m. to 11:00 p.m.

American Express, MasterCard and Visa accepted

The Cornucopia Room at Devil's Head Resort is located at the beautiful Baraboo Bluffs. It is one of the most attractive restaurants in the midwest and is only 45 minutes away from Madison. It's the best kept secret in the state of Wisconsin!

The Cornucopia was rated one of the best restaurants in the state by Isthmus of Madison. The ambiance, food and service are unmatched. Our unique menu consists of traditional French and original recipes not found anywhere. In addition, for a great getaway, our Sunday brunch is the best in the state without any doubt.

PORK OR BEEF TENDERLOINS WITH BLACKBERRY VINEGAR SAUCE

The origin of the recipe is a combination of traditional French preparation and unique ingredients. It took us about six times of mixing and combining all kinds of ingredients to come up with the conclusion.
It's very easy to prepare if the methods are followed.

		Sauce:	
14	ounces pork or beef tenderloin	4	tablespoons fresh or frozen blackberries
2	teaspoons crushed black peppercorns	1/4	cup blackberry or cider vinegar
1/4	cup plus 1 teaspoon olive oil, divided	1/4	cup sliced shallots
6	new potatoes or baby reds	1	tablespoon black currants or raisins
8	fresh baby carrots	3/4	cup beef stock
8	fresh asparagus spears	1	teaspoon cornstarch
		2	teaspoons cold water

To make sauce, soak berries in vinegar overnight. Strain the next day, pressing berries. Remove pulp and seeds. Place vinegar in saute pan, add shallots and black currants; cook until soft. Add beef stock and bring to boil. In a separate cup, mix cornstarch with cold water and add to sauce; simmer for 2 minutes.

Rub meat with crushed peppercorns. Saute meat in 1/4 cup olive oil until golden brown. Place on baking sheet and bake at 350 degrees 15-20 minutes or until desired temperature (e.g. rare, medium-rare, medium, etc.).

Peel potatoes and boil. After done, saute in 1 teaspoon of olive oil until brown. Peel and boil carrots for approximately 7 minutes. Trim ends of asparagus and boil for about 2 minutes.

Slice pork or beef about 1/2-inch thick, place at edge of plate and pour sauce over half the meat. Place asparagus over exposed meat. Place potatoes and carrots beside meat and serve. This dish goes well with a plain green salad vinaigrette.

Yields 2 servings

The
DEL BAR

The Del-Bar
800 Wisconsin Dells Parkway
PO Box 479
Lake Delton, Wisconsin 53940
608-253-1861

Open daily 4:30 p.m. to 10:00 p.m.

All major credit cards accepted

The Del-Bar, established in 1943, is a lively, spacious supper club/steakhouse serving famous custom-aged certified Angus beef and the freshest grilled seafood, with a seasonal bistro menu changing weekly. Enhance your dinner with one of our fine wines and enjoy the beautifully appointed dining rooms with wood burning fireplaces, original watercolors, and stained glass windows by nationally recognized artists.

BROILED SEA SCALLOPS VERMOUTH

The flavor of the dry sea scallops is already rich and complex,
complementing the simplicity of this dish.

6-8	large fresh dry sea scallops*
	Flour for dusting
3	tablespoons unsalted Wisconsin butter, softened
2	tablespoons sweet vermouth
1	tablespoon very fine bread crumbs

Rinse scallops quickly under cold water in colander. Dry with paper towel and dust in flour. Brush bottom of casserole dish and tops of scallops with softened butter. Pour sweet vermouth over scallops. Dust with fine bread crumbs. Bake in 400-degree oven, approximately 10 minutes. Finish under broiler until evenly browned, approximately 3 minutes.

*Dry scallops have no preservatives and are more flavorful. They are, however, very perishable and can be ordered through fine seafood retail stores.

Yields 1 serving

Garfield's Valley House
221-125th Avenue
Highway 35
Hudson, Wisconsin 54016
715-549-6255

Open Tuesday through Thursday 12:00 p.m. to 10:00 p.m.

Friday and Saturday 12:00 a.m. to 2:00 a.m.

Sunday 12:00 p.m. to 8:00 p.m.

Diner's Club, MasterCard and Visa accepted

Garfield's Valley House has been under the same ownership since 1988. Our primary business is weddings, banquets, and large groups. We also offer a full menu which includes steaks and seafood. Our hamburgers are considered the best in the St. Croix Valley.

PAUL'S BLUE CHEESE DRESSING

This is our most asked for dressing!
For a lighter recipe, use light mayonnaise and/or light sour cream.
Refrigerated, this dressing will last up to three weeks.

2	cups mayonnaise
1	cup Wisconsin sour cream
2	tablespoons grated Wisconsin Parmesan cheese
1-2	cloves garlic, minced
1	teaspoon Worcestershire sauce
$1/2$	cup Wisconsin buttermilk
$1/2$	teaspoon salt
$1/2$	teaspoon (scant) white pepper
2	tablespoons minced onion
3	ounces Wisconsin Blue cheese, crumbled

In medium bowl, combine all ingredients, except Blue cheese. With wire whisk, mix for 3 minutes or until smooth. Fold in Blue cheese.

Yields 8 servings

GEORGE WILLIAMS COLLEGE EDUCATIONAL CENTERS | LAKE GENEVA CAMPUS

George Williams College Educational Centers
Lake Geneva Campus
350 North Lake Shore Drive
PO Box 210
Williams Bay, Wisconsin 53191
414-245-5531

Open daily 7:30 a.m. to 9:00 a.m.
11:30 a.m. to 1:00 p.m.
5:15 p.m. to 6:30 p.m.

Our campus is the site of one of the largest resident outdoor and environmental education centers in the United States. Our diverse staff, ranging in age from 14 to senior citizens, serves about 300,000 meals a year. Our two beautiful dining rooms can serve up to 600 people at one time. The meals, served mainly buffet-style, are wholesome, nutritious, "home cooked" foods, and we always offer something vegetarian.

The beautiful lake-side setting of the Lake Geneva campus has proven to be an excellent location for personal and professional growth programs. Many of the over 30,000 participants return annually for a variety of educational, religious or human service programs. The campus is also a gathering place for families to relax and renew relationships and just enjoy the Lake Geneva campus on their own.

BROCCOLI LASAGNA

It's convenient!
It can be made a day ahead and stored in your refrigerator.
It's low-fat, and it's delicious. Even those who don't care for broccoli
will love this lasagna, which was developed by Chef Jim Christiansen
from another recipe as an alternative to traditional tomato sauce lasagna.

1	16-ounce bag shredded Wisconsin Mozzarella cheese; divided
2	16-ounce containers low-fat Wisconsin cottage cheese
1/4	cup grated Wisconsin Parmesan cheese
1/4	cup dried, whole oregano
1 1/2	teaspoons garlic powder
1	single serving Egg Beaters (2 eggs)
2	10 3/4-ounce cans Campbells Healthy Request Cream of Broccoli Soup (condensed)
16	lasagna noodles, uncooked
1/2	cup shredded carrot
1/3	cup finely diced onion
1	10-ounce package frozen cut broccoli (thawed)

In a chilled bowl, mix half of Mozzarella cheese with cottage cheese, Parmesan cheese, oregano, garlic powder, and Egg Beaters. Set aside, keeping cheese and egg mixture at or below 40 degrees until ready to bake.

In chilled, well greased 9 x 13-inch baking pan, spread 1/2 cup of soup and top with 4 lasagna noodles. Spread 1/2 of cheese and egg mixture, carrots and onions and top with 4 noodles; press down firmly. Spread 1 cup of soup over noodles. Add cut broccoli; top with 4 noodles, firmly pressing. Spread remaining cheese mixture, top with 4 noodles. Spread remaining soup and top with remaining Mozzarella cheese.

Bake at 375 degrees for 1 1/2 hours, tenting pan with foil so cheese on top won't stick. Let stand 10 minutes before cutting.

Yields 10 servings

The Goose Blind, etc.
512 Gold Street
Green Lake, Wisconsin 54941
414-294-6363

Open daily from 11:00 a.m.

Discover, MasterCard and Visa accepted

Green Lake, one of Wisconsin's most beautiful vacation destinations, is a Mecca for outdoor recreation enthusiasts of all kinds. The Goose Blind is a haven for these hungry and thirsty enthusiasts who "flock" in after a long day of boating, golfing, or fishing the waters of the deepest lake in the state. From the trophy walleye mounted in the bar to the vintage photographs of the Green Lake area decorating the dining room, The Goose Blind reflects the charm and friendliness of rural Wisconsin at its best.

Jeff and Mary Rowley have owned and operated The Goose Blind, etc. since 1985, adding an expanded dining room, banquet facilities, and an outdoor patio to the original building. On the patio, summertime patrons might choose to enjoy a traditional Wisconsin fish boil or just sip a cocktail while the kids play at the LEGO table or ride the mechanical horse. Whether the order of the day calls for a Signature Pizza and a cold pitcher of beer, or a sampling of lunch and dinner entrees ranging from stir-frys to Southwestern favorites, The Goose Blind offers fun and family enjoyment in a comfortable, casual setting.

GOOSE BLIND CHILI

The Goose Blind Chili recipe featured here won the best spice award at the Wisconsin State Chili Cook-off in 1991.

2¹/₂	pounds ground beef
1	large onion, diced
1	green pepper, diced
4	stalks celery, sliced
1	tablespoon oil
2	teaspoons crushed garlic
1	tablespoon chili powder
1	teaspoon black pepper
1	teaspoon cumin
1	teaspoon crushed red pepper flakes
1	teaspoon seasoned salt
	Pinch of basil
	Pinch of thyme
1	28-ounce can tomato puree
1	28-ounce can diced tomatoes
1	28-ounce can kidney beans
1	16-ounce can tomato juice

In large stockpot, brown ground beef; drain. In separate pan, saute vegetables in oil and seasonings. When vegetables are tender and onion is translucent, blend in with beef. Add canned items and allow to simmer at least 1 hour.

Optional: For hotter chili with a Southwestern twist, add a few tablespoons of diced jalapeno peppers during the simmering process.

Yields 12-15 servings

The Grandview
Restaurant & Lounge

The Grandview Restaurant and Lounge
The Geneva Inn
N2009 State Road 120
Lake Geneva, Wisconsin 53147
414-248-5690

Open lunch Monday through Saturday
11:30 a.m. to 2:30 p.m.

Sunday brunch 10:30 a.m. to 2:00 p.m.

Dinner Monday through Saturday from 5:00 p.m.
Sunday from 3:00 p.m.

All major credit cards accepted

Perhaps one of the area's better-kept secrets of corporate as well as romantic pleasures is the Geneva Inn, built by owners Clarence and Marilyn Schawk, Chicago residents who have always summered at the lake. Nostalgia prompted the couple to buy the property, located just outside of town on the south shore of the almost eight-mile-long lake, once occupied by the old Shore Club where they used to dine.

Dining in the Grandview Restaurant is always an occasion and care is bestowed on the room so that every table has a view of the winking lights across the still, dark water. The Geneva Inn is the only property of its kind that sits without interruption on the lake, and has a 30-foot drop with a long flight of steps leading directly to its own dock and marina.

Dinners at the Grandview Restaurant start with such appetizers as Caesar salad with shrimp or a wild mushroom strudel, followed by a selection of entrees like a tender rack of lamb or tournedos with three-peppercorn sauce. Fresh fish might include red snapper, grouper, or the popular Pacific Northwest salmon delivered daily from Chicago, along with the shellfish that go into an excellent cioppino served with herb-roasted French bread. The tempting dessert tray offers a choice of berries in season, fresh fruit tarts, and inn favorites like the rich, dark chocolate pie or the creamy cheesecake.

GRILLED STUFFED BUTTERFLIED PORK LOIN
WITH HONEY PEAR CREAM SAUCE

*Chef Henry Hys first offered this as a dinner special during the
Christmas season. The pork loin was so well received that we will
certainly be offering it again. To get the best flavor for the sauce,
the pears should be very ripe. A chardonnay or gewurztraminer
would complement this dish nicely.*

4	6-ounce pork loins
1	pound mushrooms
1	medium onion
1	clove garlic
1-2	tablespoons olive oil, to taste
	Salt and pepper to taste

Sauce:

1	16-ounce bottle of white wine
4	cups Wisconsin heavy cream
2	tablespoons honey
3-4	ripe pears, peeled and diced to 1/4-inch
	Salt and pepper to taste

Butterfly each pork loin. On inside of each half, cut pockets for filling. Set aside.

Chop mushrooms, onion, and garlic to a fine dice. Saute onion and garlic in oil until
translucent, then add mushrooms. Season with salt and pepper to taste. Let mixture cool.
When mixture is cool, stuff each pocket of the pork loin.

For the sauce, pour wine into a heavy-bottomed pot and cook slowly until reduced to
syrup consistency. Whisk in heavy cream, honey, and pears. Season with salt and pepper.

Sear grill marks on both sides of pork loin, 2 minutes on each side. Finish in 500-
degree convection oven for 5 minutes. Check doneness by slightly opening the butterfly
to observe color of the meat. Serve with Honey Pear Cream Sauce.

Yields 4 servings

Grenadier's

Grenadier's Restaurant, Inc.
747 North Broadway
Milwaukee, Wisconsin 53202
414-276-0747

*Open Monday through Friday,
lunch from 11:30 a.m. to 2:30 p.m.*

*Monday through Saturday,
dinner from 5:30 p.m. to 10:30 p.m.*

All major credit cards accepted

Grenadier's consists of four distinct dining rooms, each offering a different elegant setting. We offer French-continental cuisine with fresh seafood, game, fowl, lamb, and beef and feature daily specialties for both lunch and dinner. Our Degustation Menu is offered weekly, and we have a Wine Spectator award-winning wine cellar. We have a number of French red and white burgundies as well as a great selection of red French bordeauxs. Grenadier's has been the recipient of the Mobil 4-Star rating for the last 13 years. With complimentary valet parking nightly, Grenadier's is located in downtown Milwaukee, just east of the river.

FRESH SEA SCALLOPS IN A SESAME SEED CRUST

*At Grenadier's we serve this low fat dish with black linguine,
but the pasta of your choice may be substituted.*

16	large fresh sea scallops
1	cup sesame seeds
1/2	cup olive or sesame oil, divided
2	cups diced scallions
2	cups diced fresh tomato
1/2	cup chutney
1/4	cup diced cilantro
1/4	cup lime juice
	Pasta of your choice
1	cup oyster sauce

Turn sea scallops in sesame seeds. Heat 1/4 cup oil in pan and lightly saute scallops until light golden brown. In a separate pan, quickly saute scallions in remaining 1/4 cup oil. Add tomatoes, chutney and cilantro and finish with lime juice. Set the panache on a prewarmed plate and top it with sea scallops. Set pasta in center of plate and lightly drizzle with oyster sauce.

Yields 4 servings

Wausau's Most Unique Water Front Restaurant

Gulliver's Landing Waterfront Restaurant
2204 Rib Mountain Drive
Wausau, Wisconsin 54401
715-842-9098

Open daily 4:30 p.m. to 10:00 p.m.

Closed all major holidays

All major credit cards accepted

Gulliver's Landing Waterfront Restaurant was established in May, 1984 by Allan and Lori Woldt, local Rib Mountaineers. Allan, who has been in the hospitality business for 24 years, wanted to open a restaurant where the guests were assured the highest quality food at a reasonable price, while enjoying Wausau's most unique nautical atmosphere. As you walk through our nautical gift shop, two dining rooms, lounge, banquet facility, outdoor veranda, and lawns, you will enjoy all the nautical memorabilia.

Our menu features seafood, steaks, cajun foods, and ribs.

SHRIMP STUFFED CHICKEN BREAST

*A unique combination of land and sea
that complement one another perfectly.*

Stuffing:
- 8 ounces salad shrimp, cooked
- 1 cup 1/2-inch diced Wisconsin Swiss cheese
- 1/2 cup sliced green onions
- 4 tablespoons mayonnaise
- 1 teaspoon dill weed

- 4 8-ounce fresh boneless, skinless chicken breasts
- 4 tablespoons Wisconsin butter, melted
- 1 teaspoon seasoned salt
- 1 teaspoon paprika
- 4 cups cooked instant wild rice

Mix stuffing ingredients in a 2-quart mixing bowl. Wrap each chicken breast around 1/4 of stuffing mixture. Place stuffed chicken breasts in greased 2-quart casserole dish. Top with melted butter, seasoned salt, and paprika. Bake uncovered at 375 degrees for 30 minutes.

Using a large spoon, place cooked, stuffed chicken breasts on top of wild rice.

Yields 4 servings

Hi-Way Restaurant
2767 Highway 41-141
Abrams, Wisconsin 54101
414-826-5900

Open daily 4:00 a.m. to 11:00 p.m.

Discover, MasterCard and Visa accepted

The Hi-Way Restaurant was opened in 1982 on US Highway 41-141 in Abrams, Wisconsin. A few months later the Fuel Station was added. In April of 1992, Century 21 Van Jantzen Real Estate was opened on the north wing of the Hi-Way Restaurant. And in August of 1993, the Hi-Way Travel Mart opened for business.

Due to the dedication of over 70 employees the restaurant, Fuel Station, and Travel Mart provide our customers with a friendly atmosphere. We welcome you to come and try our daily specials, delicious homemade pies, and soups.

HI-WAY RESTAURANT PIE CRUST

Each day, long-time employees Florence and Elaine bake up dozens of tasty pies for our customers. Over 150 pieces are served on weekdays and over 300 per day on weekends! This pie crust is used in some of our most requested pies, such as sour cream raisin and banana cream.

2 cups flour
$1/3$ cup Wisconsin milk
$1/4$ teaspoon salt
$2/3$ cup cooking oil
Dash of baking powder

Mix all ingredients together in a medium bowl until a semi-firm dough is formed. Roll out to $1/4$-inch thickness between 2 sheets of plastic or wax paper. Line 9-inch pie tin with 1 crust. Top pie with the second crust.

Bake according to time and temperature guide on your filling.

Yields 2 crusts

Irish Waters
702 North Whitney Way
Madison, Wisconsin 53705
608-233-3398

Open Monday through Saturday 11:00 a.m. to 11:00 p.m.

Sundays Noon to 11:00 p.m.

Discover, MasterCard and Visa accepted

Irish Waters was established 16 years ago by the late Mike Campion. He built the original building in the style of a turn-of-the-century Irish pub due to the love and pride of his Irish heritage.

A two-sided fireplace greets you as you enter the restaurant, taking a chill off from these Wisconsin winters. The interior is decorated with rich, dark oak booths and tables tastefully accented with stained glass and brass. As you work your way to the large mahogany bar, which dominates the center area of the restaurant, you feel the comfortable ambiance of the decor.

Grab a pint of Guinness or an Irish coffee and step out to the Garden Room. General seating or private party arrangements can be made, if you desire, for the Garden Room.

The menu features home-style soups, salads, gourmet sandwiches and specialty burgers. Dinners range from fish and chips to tenderloin steaks. We offer daily lunch and dinner specials for your enjoyment. Every Wednesday is Irish Fest, featuring our house specialty, Corned Beef and Cabbage Dinner, as well as other traditional delicacies such as Irish Stew, Irish Soda Bread and Cream of Potato Soup.

Join us on St. Patrick's Day for the largest party in town. (Be forewarned that this party is not for the faint of heart.) The celebration is only limited by your imagination or the amount of blarney you're willing to accept. So come party with the Irish—no one does it better...

Irish Waters is located at the corner of University Avenue at Whitney Way, merely 10 minutes from the state capital.

Good food, good cheer, good friends, the Irish way!

IRISH WATERS IRISH STEW

Fills the stomach and warms the soul as any good Irish cooking will do!

1¼	pounds boneless lamb stew meat, cubed, uncooked
	Dash of salt and pepper
1⅛	teaspoons crushed garlic
2¼	teaspoons corn oil
¼	cup cooking sherry
3	cups chicken broth
1⅓	cups Spanish onions, coarsely chopped
¾	teaspoon Worcestershire sauce
⅓	teaspoon thyme
½	teaspoon garlic salt
½	teaspoon ground white pepper
¾	teaspoon ground allspice
1	bay leaf
2	cups carrots, coarsely chopped
1½	baking potatoes, peeled and coarsely chopped
1	cup chopped green cabbage
¼	cup flour
1¼	tablespoons cornstarch
½	cup water
¼	teaspoon Kitchen Bouquet

Brown lamb stew meat in salt and pepper, garlic and corn oil. Add cooking sherry, chicken broth, onion and spices. Bring to boil, reduce heat and simmer 45 minutes. Add carrots and simmer 15 minutes. Add potatoes and simmer 10 minutes. Add cabbage and simmer 5 minutes. Dissolve flour and cornstarch in water; add to stew. Let thicken and add kitchen bouquet, simmering another 5 minutes. Serve hot.

Yields 8 servings

The Inn at

KRISTOFER'S

The Inn at Kristofer's
734 Bayshore Drive
Sister Bay, Wisconsin 54234-0619
414-854-9419

*Open daily May through October lunch from 11:30 a.m.
dinner from 5:30 p.m.*

*November through April open Thursday through Sunday
lunch from 11:30 a.m., dinner from 5:30 p.m.*

MasterCard and Visa accepted

Located directly across from the village marina in downtown Sister Bay, The Inn at Kristofer's offers distinctive midwestern fare at Door County's newest restaurant and only cooking school.

Lunch and dinner are complemented by an espresso cafe. Guests enjoy the expansive view of the Green Bay waters from the Inn's dining room. Handcrafted pine tables grace the restaurant's dining room. Each table is set with antique silver and complemented by depression glass creamer and sugar.

Guests at the Inn at Kristofer's can unwind at the end of the day with a favorite wine or beer and choose from a variety of simple yet elegant entrees such as Salmon with Champagne Sauce or Grilled Herb Duck Breast with Wild Rice. Dine fireside on cool autumn evenings or deckside on warm summer days. Chef/co-owner Terri Milligan also offers cooking demonstrations on regional cooking techniques throughout the year. The Inn at Kristofer's is open year-round.

DUCK BREAST SALAD WITH HONEY HAZELNUT VINAIGRETTE DRESSING

One of the most requested recipes at The Inn at Kristofer's is our house dressing. At the restaurant, we serve our house dressing on fresh greens with Granny Smith apples and toasted pine nuts. The dressing is also wonderful on our Duck Breast Salad with Pears. The duck breast salad makes a wonderful luncheon or light dinner entree.

		Honey Hazelnut Dressing:
6	boneless duck breasts	$1/4$ teaspoon salt
2	tablespoons olive oil	Dash of white pepper
1	cup pea pods, cleaned	2 cloves garlic, crushed
3	carrots, peeled and julienne sliced	$1/4$ cup honey
2	heads red leaf lettuce, cleaned and torn into large bite-sized pieces	$1/3$ cup white wine vinegar
		2 teaspoons good quality Dijon mustard
3	ripe pears	2 teaspoons hazelnut oil
		$1^{1}/4$ cups extra virgin olive oil

Remove skin from duck breasts. In large saute pan, over medium-high heat, place olive oil. Add duck breasts and lightly saute until medium (still pink in the center), approximately 5-6 minutes per side. Set aside and cool.

In a pot of boiling water, blanch pea pods (approximately 1 minute) and cool under cold water. Blanch carrots in the same manner. In large serving bowl, place cleaned leaf lettuce, carrots, and pea pods. Toss lightly to combine. Divide tossed salad on 6 large serving plates. On cutting board, thinly slice duck breast. Place slices from one duck breast on each salad plate, arranging them decoratively on greens. Peel and core pears. Slice pears thinly and place slices around rim of each plate. Drizzle Honey Hazelnut Dressing on each plated salad and serve.

To make dressing, in a large bowl, combine salt, white pepper, mashed garlic cloves, honey, vinegar, and mustard. Whisk to combine. Slowly whisk in hazelnut oil. In a very slow trickle, add olive oil while continually whisking mixture. Be careful not to add oil too quickly or dressing will separate.

Yields 6 servings

Karl Ratzsch's

THE IMPRESSIVE GERMAN RESTAURANT

Karl Ratzsch's Restaurant
320 East Mason Street
Milwaukee, Wisconsin 53202
414-276-2720

Open Monday through Friday
3:00 p.m. to 9:30 p.m.

Saturday 3:00 p.m. to 10:30 p.m.

Sunday 3:00 a.m. to 9:00 p.m.

All major credit cards accepted

This history of Karl Ratzsch's Restaurant goes back as far as 1904 when chef Otto Herman opened a small cafe in downtown Milwaukee. A few years later, his step-daughter, Helen, came from Germany to live with him in quarters above the cafe.

Just prior to World War I, Karl Ratzsch Sr. took a tour of the United States and found himself stranded due to the outbreak of war. Eventually, Karl made his way to Milwaukee where he took a job at Otto Herman's Cafe. After a ten-year courtship, he married Helen and bought the cafe.

In 1929, Karl and Helen relocated the business to its present location and named it The Old Heidelberg Cafe. The country was in the grip of depression during those early years, but Karl an Helen managed to establish a loyal following. Helen, affectionately known as "Mama Ratzsch," began filling the restaurant with her beautiful collection of steins, porcelain and glassware from Europe. To avoid confusion with other German restaurants, the name was changed to Karl Ratzsch's Restaurant in the early thirties.

Karl and Helen continued to be active in the operation of the restaurant their years, but Karl Ratzsch Jr. took on the main responsibility late in the fifties. Under his guidance, the restaurant grew in popularity, and continues today in the traditions of quality and old world elegance established by his parents.

SEARED LOIN OF LAMB

*Enjoy this lamb loin garnished with a mint leaf
and served with rice pilaf and salted green beans.*

16	ounces lamb loin, trimmed
1	teaspoon fresh lemon juice
2	tablespoons olive oil, divided
2	teaspoons crushed garlic
1	teaspoon oregano
	Black pepper and salt to taste

Sauce:

3	tablespoons plus $1/2$ teaspoon softened Wisconsin butter
$1/2$	teaspoon flour
$1/2$	cup Port wine
1	tablespoon currant jelly
$1^1/2$	cups light beef stock
1	teaspoon Dijon mustard

Rub loin of lamb on both sides with lemon juice, 1 tablespoon of the olive oil, garlic, oregano, black pepper, and salt. Cover and refrigerate overnight.

Sear lamb loin in saute pan with remaining olive oil over medium-high heat, about 4 minutes on each side. Remove lamb and finish cooking in 300-degree oven to desired internal temperature.

In small saucepan, combine $1/2$ teaspoon butter and flour to make roux; cook 5 minutes, stirring occasionally. Set aside. Deglaze saute pan used to sear lamb with wine, jelly, and beef stock. On high heat, reduce to 1 cup and whip in roux. Reduce heat to low and simmer. Remove from stove and whip in mustard and remaining 3 tablespoons butter; adjust seasoning if needed. Strain sauce through cheese cloth. To serve, spoon sauce on plate, slice lamb in $1/4$-inch slices, and fan out over sauce.

Yields 3 servings

Kavanaughs' Esquire Club
1025 North Sherman Avenue
Madison, Wisconsin 53704
608-249-0193

Open Monday through Friday lunch 11:00 a.m. to 3:00 p.m.

Dinner Monday through Thursday 4:00 p.m. to 10:00 p.m.
Friday 4:00 p.m. to 11:00 p.m.
Saturday 11:00 a.m. to 10:30 p.m.
Sunday Noon to 9:30 p.m.

All major credit cards accepted

As Madison's oldest continually operated family owned restaurant, Kavanaughs' Esquire Club has long been offering food which satisfies its customers. During this time, customers of 40 years, a constant stream of new customers and an occasional past or current governor have enjoyed the food and atmosphere of Kavanaughs'.

Serving the state's capital since 1947, Kavanaughs' was one of the first to introduce a fish fry to Wisconsin. Today, with the third generation of Kavanaughs at the helm, the ever-popular fish fry is still prepared. In addition to great seafood, Kavanaughs' is a certified Angus beef house and features excellent steaks. All these favorites are served in the relaxed familiar atmosphere which continues to make Kavanaughs' Esquire Club a favorite gathering spot.

MINT TORTE

This recipe is a special favorite of a special lady, Jane Kavanaugh, of the first generation Kavanaughs. Thank you Mom/Grandma.

———————————————— ⊂══▷ ————————————————

3/4	cup Wisconsin butter, divided	3	1-ounce squares unsweetened chocolate, melted
2	cups vanilla wafer crumbs	2	cups Wisconsin whipping cream
1 1/2	cups powdered sugar, sifted	1	10 1/2-ounce package miniature marshmallows
3	eggs, lightly beaten	1/2	cup crushed peppermint candy

Melt 1/4 cup of butter and blend together with crumbs. Press firmly in bottom of a greased 8-inch square pan. Cream together remaining butter and powdered sugar thoroughly. Add eggs and melted chocolate. Beat until light and fluffy and spoon over crumbs. Place in freezer.

Meanwhile, whip cream until soft peaks form. Fold marshmallows into whipped cream. Remove pan from freezer and spread marshmallow mixture over chocolate layer. Sprinkle with crushed candy. Freeze before serving if you wish.

Yields 12 servings

BEER & CHEESE SPREAD

Since the 1960s when it was brought to Kavanaughs' by a member of the staff, this spread has been featured at the restaurant and is a favorite of our guests.

2	cups shredded, sharp Wisconsin Cheddar cheese	1/2	teaspoon dry mustard
2	cups shredded Wisconsin Swiss cheese	1	small clove garlic, minced
1	teaspoon Worcestershire sauce	1/2-2/3	cup beer

Combine cheese, Worcestershire sauce, mustard, and garlic. Beat in enough beer to make spreading consistency.

Serve on assorted crackers or rye bread.

Yields 2 cups

The Kennedy Manor Dining Room & Bar
1 Langdon Street
Madison, Wisconsin 53703
608-256-5556

Open Tuesday through Saturday

Lunch 11:00 a.m. to 2:00 p.m.

Dinner 5:30 p.m. to 10:00 p.m.

MasterCard and Visa accepted

In an historic Madison neighborhood, close to the UW campus and the Capitol Square, The Kennedy Manor Dining Room & Bar is a half-flight downstairs in a lovely old apartment building, vintage 1930. A Christy & Craig Associates Restaurant, The Kennedy Manor is intimate, timeless, and soothing. The food is simple, beautifully prepared and European-inspired. The restaurant features a moderately price European wine list and excellent breads. The dinner menu changes daily but standards include Oven Roasted Chicken, with handmade mashed potatoes; risotto, freshly made throughout the evening; Osso Bucco; Fresh Salmon and Sorrel Sauce; and Beef Tenderloin. Fresh fruit ices, Chocolate Steamed Pudding, and Spanish Orange Custard are favorite desserts. The bar is great, and remembered nostalgically by UW grads of seven decades.

Parking: Evenings after 4:30 p.m., all day and evening on the weekend. Parking courtesy of neighboring businesses, Grant Thornton Accounting and National Guardian Life Insurance. The GT lot is directly across the street from the restaurant, contiguous to The Edgewater Hotel.

CHOCOLATE STEAMED PUDDING

The old-fashioned method of baking cakes—steaming—is so old-fashioned it's simple. And it results in a moist, dense, rich cake that makes this dessert our most requested at The Kennedy Manor.

9	ounces bittersweet chocolate
3/4	cup unsalted Wisconsin butter
6	eggs, separated
1	cup granulated white sugar, divided
1/4	cup all-purpose flour

Combine chocolate and butter in bowl over a water bath/double boiler and melt slowly over low-simmering water. When melted, thoroughly combine and pull off the heat.

In a separate bowl, beat egg whites on high speed until foamy. Add 1/2 cup sugar and continue to beat the whites until soft peaks form and hold. Remove bowl from mixer and put aside.

In a third bowl, beat egg yolks on high and slowly add remaining 1/2 cup sugar. Continue to beat until the volume triples, the color is light yellow, and the sugar has dissolved. Add the melted chocolate/butter mixture and beat until thoroughly blended.

Add flour to mixture and beat on low to blend, then beat on high for 10 seconds. Turn the mixer down to low again and begin to add the already beaten egg whites to the chocolate mixture. Combine thoroughly. Stop the mixer, detach the bowl and scrape along the sides and bottom of bowl to make sure that you have incorporated all of the chocolate.

This mixture can be stored in the refrigerator at this point for two days, or baked immediately in 6 4-ounce heat-resistant custard cups, or in one 9x1-inch cake pan. Fill cups or pan to the rim and level. Place the cake inside a roasting pan or larger cake pan. Fill this larger pan with 1 inch warm water. Cover and seal with metal foil, allowing 2 inches above cake to rise. Either place on the stove top on medium-high heat until you hear the water boiling, then turn heat to low for 30 minutes or place in 325-degree oven for 45 minutes. Be careful on the stove top not to let the water boil away: add more water as needed or turn temperature down. While cooking, the cake will swell and expand 1 to 2 inches above the rim but will deflate upon cooling.

Loosen the cake around the edge with a knife and invert onto plate to serve. Serve with fresh vanilla ice cream and your favorite chocolate sauce. Garnish with mint.

Yields 6 servings

Leffel's
Supper Club

Leffel's Supper Club
1315 Forrest Avenue
Antigo, Wisconsin 54409
715-627-7027

*Open Monday through Friday
Lunch 11:00 a.m. to 2:00 p.m.*

*Dinner Monday through Saturday
5:00 p.m. to 10:00 p.m.*

*Sunday Brunch 11:00 a.m. to 2:00 p.m.
and dinner 4:00 p.m. to 10:00 p.m.*

Discover, MasterCard and Visa, accepted

Leffel's Supper Club has offered fine dining and hospitality for 30 years. We are known for our efficient crew who take care of large parties as well as accommodate the appetites waiting in the main dining room. Our rustic turn-of-the century lodge is located on the southern edge of Antigo on County Y, just 1/2 mile from Highway 45, in a setting of stately pines and blue spruce trees.

We offer new and different entrees every day and night of the week. Our prime rib is known throughout the state as the most tender and delicious anywhere. On Wednesday nights we feature a Gourmet Night with a special menu that is out of this world.

Our regular menu has a vast selection of steak, chicken and seafood dishes.

TOURNEDOS MANCARELLA

This recipe began in a little continental restaurant in Connecticut and was brought together here in the midwest—the northwoods of Wisconsin. I believe it is a simple entree that adds a culinary touch to any occasion— to impress friends; for an elegant dinner; or just to romance the palate. We hope you enjoy.

Sun-dried Tomato Vinaigrette:
2	cups water
1/2	cup sun-dried tomatoes
1	cup virgin olive oil
1/4	cup balsamic vinegar
1/8	cup red wine vinegar
3/4	tablespoon fresh oregano, chopped
1	teaspoon fresh garlic, minced
1/8	teaspoon salt
1/8	teaspoon black pepper

4	tablespoons clarified Wisconsin butter or vegetable oil
8	5-ounce beef tenderloin filets
	Salt and black pepper to taste
8	ounces Wisconsin Gorgonzola cheese, crumbled
4	sprigs fresh oregano for garnish

To make vinaigrette, boil water in saucepan. Blanch sun-dried tomatoes for 2 minutes; drain and let cool. Chop tomatoes and put in mixing bowl. Add oil, vinegars, oregano, garlic, salt, and pepper; whisk well. Refrigerate at least 2 hours. Remove from refrigerator about 30 minutes before serving and bring to room temperature.

To prepare tenderloin, add butter or oil to pan. Season beef on both sides with salt and pepper and cook uncovered on high to desired doneness. (Note: about 2 minutes on each side for medium-rare.) Remove from heat and top each filet with 1 ounce of Gorgonzola cheese. Place under broiler for 30 seconds to melt cheese.

Mix vinaigrette well and pour an equal amount over each filet. Put 2 filets on each plate, garnish with oregano sprig, and serve.

Yields 4 servings

Millie's

Millie's Restaurants and Shopping Village
N2484 County O
Delavan, Wisconsin 53115
414-728-2434

Open 8:00 a.m. to 4:00 p.m.
Tuesday through Sunday

July and August daily

January and February Saturday and Sunday only

Millie's Restaurants and Shopping Village was founded in September of 1964 by Mildred Novak. She and her family operated the business until 1980 when Millie sold it to her very good friend, Kitty Slater. Millie's thrived as Kitty and her family continued to offer delicious food in a unique and charming environment. In 1994, Kitty retired and passed the mantle over to her son and daughter-in-law. Bill and Maureen Slater are continuing to follow the traditions of quality established by Millie over 30 years ago.

Millie's is located on 7 acres of rich Wisconsin farmland with lush English gardens and a lovely Victorian gazebo.

Old-fashioned recipes make a trip to Millie's an unforgettable experience. Each item is served by an experienced, courteous staff member who is determined to make your visit memorable.

Enjoy the entire complex: restaurant, shops and beautifully landscaped grounds. Stop for a cocktail in the Courtyard Lounge and visit one of the five gracious dining rooms where antiques abound.

Following your meal, five unique boutiques, including Millie's own Gift Haus, await your browsing. Each specialty shop is filled with new ideas and merchandise to fit any occasion and budget.

Millie's is just 15 minutes from Lake Geneva and is close enough to Madison, Milwaukee and Chicago to make it the perfect destination for a leisurely day in the country.

CHICKEN SPAETZLE SOUP

This soup continues to be a favorite of Millie's patrons.
Its home-style goodness makes it a perfect accompaniment to any meal.

Chicken Stock:
12	cups water
4	pounds chicken, cut up
1	large onion, chopped
3	carrots, sliced
2	celery stalks, chopped
1	tablespoon salt
6	sprigs parsley
2	sprigs thyme
2	bay leaves
4	peppercorns
	Additional salt to taste

Spaetzle:
3	cups sifted flour
1	teaspoon salt
$1/8$	teaspoon nutmeg
$1/8$	teaspoon white pepper
3	eggs, slightly beaten
1	cup water

In large kettle, bring water to a boil. Add chicken and skim off froth as it rises to the surface; lower heat to simmer. Add onion, carrots, celery, and salt. Make bouquet garni by placing parsley, thyme, bay leaves and peppercorns in piece of cheesecloth. Tie string around cloth to make a pouch. Add pouch to boiling water. Cover kettle and simmer for about $1^1/2$ hours.

Remove chicken from kettle. Remove meat from carcass, reserving meat, if you like, for another use. Return carcass to kettle and continue to simmer for about 1 hour. Remove carcass and bouquet garni. Strain stock and add salt to taste.

To make spaetzles, combine flour, salt, nutmeg, and pepper in medium bowl. Add eggs and water; mix well. Spoon out dough and cut small pieces with knife into rapidly boiling salted water. Spaetzles are done when they float to the top. Remove them with slotted spoon and add to hot prepared chicken stock.

Serve Chicken Spaetzle Soup garnished with fresh chopped parsley.

Yields 8-10 servings

New Glarus Hotel
100 Sixth Avenue
New Glarus, Wisconsin 53574
608-527-5244

Open daily May 1 through November 1

Sunday through Thursday 11:00 a.m. to 9:00 p.m.
Friday and Saturday 11:00 a.m. to 10:00 p.m.

November 1 through May 1

Lunch daily 11:00 a.m. to 2:00 p.m.
Dinner Sunday through Thursday
5:00 p.m. to 8:00 p.m.
Friday and Saturday 5:00 p.m. to 10:00 p.m.

All major credit cards accepted

For over 20 years the New Glarus Hotel has set the standards for the best Swiss cuisine in the area. Patrons return again and again to experience both the fine food and the gemutlichkeit of its festive Swiss atmosphere.

Enjoy authentic Swiss cuisine in our air-conditioned dining room or dine on our popular balcony overlooking downtown New Glarus. Special group and bus menus are also available.

Dine and dance every Friday and Saturday night year-round to the music of the famous Roger Bright Polka Band.

The restaurant is located in downtown New Glarus—America's Little Switzerland—it's close to home, just a short drive from Madison, Chicago, and Milwaukee; but it's like taking a mini-vacation to Europe. We hope to see you soon!

CHEESE FONDUE

*It is an old tradition, that if a person loses their piece of bread in the fondue,
he or she must kiss the person to the right of him or her!*

*A cup of tea goes well with fondue and aids digestion.
Fresh fruit makes a good dessert.*

½	pound Wisconsin Swiss cheese
½	pound Wisconsin Gruyere cheese
1	rounded tablespoon flour
2	loaves crusty Italian or French bread
1	clove garlic
1½	cups dry white wine
1	tablespoon lemon juice
	Pepper and nutmeg to taste

Grate, shred or if using slices, finely dice Swiss and Gruyere cheese. Dredge cheese
with flour. You can do this in advance and keep the cheese refrigerated in a tightly closed
plastic bag. Cut bread into 1-inch cubes. Each cube should have crust on one side.

Rub inside of pot with cut garlic clove. Place pot on stove. Pour wine into pot. Heat
over medium flame until wine is hot but not boiling. Add lemon juice. Add handfuls of
cheese, stirring constantly with a wooden spoon until cheese is melted and the cheese-
wine mixture has the appearance of a light creamy sauce. Add pepper and nutmeg to
taste. Bring to a boil then remove pot and place on lighted burner on top of table.

Adjust flame of burner so fondue continues bubbling very lightly. Serve each guest a
handful of bread cubes from a plate or basket. Spear fork through soft part of bread first,
securing prongs into crust. Dunk to bottom of pot and stir well. Remove fork and twist
over pot.

Yields 4 servings as main course and 12-24 as an appetizer

The Norske Nook

in the ♥ of Osseo

The Norske Nook
207 West 7th Street
PO Box 213
Osseo, Wisconsin 54758
715-597-3069-restaurant
715-597-3688-bakery

Open Monday through Saturday 5:30 a.m. to 9:30 p.m.

Sunday 10:00 am. to 4:00 p.m.

The Norske Nook is located in downtown Osseo, Wisconsin, 20 miles south of Eau Claire off Interstate 90.

The restaurant was purchased in 1990 by owner Jerry Bechard. He has maintained the same old-fashioned home cooking and friendly service that customers had experienced previously.

In January of 1994, a new Norske Nook Bakery and Restaurant opened for business seven days a week. It offers a full menu, plus a variety of favorite bakery items made from scratch, namely breads, cookies, muffins, donuts, decorated cakes, jam, pies and a variety of Norwegian treats.

Many tour buses here in the midwest make this a must-stop. Polls taken have decided that the Norske Nook makes the best desserts in the midwest.

Coming in mid-June of 1995, another Norske Nook Bakery and Restaurant will be opening in Rice Lake, Wisconsin. We're always pleased to welcome you to stop and try a traditional favorite.

CHOCOLATE MOUSSE PIE

At The Norske Nook, owner Jerry Bechard and his staff
enjoy trying new things, especially creating new pie varieties.
This recipe is one of their creations that is now a favorite of customers too.

5	cups heavy Wisconsin whipping cream
1½	teaspoons vanilla
2	cups powdered sugar
¾	cups dry chocolate pudding mix
3	tablespoons cocoa
3½	cups whipped topping, divided
1	10-inch crust, baked
1	tablespoon shaved semi-sweet chocolate

Mix cream and vanilla together in a large electric mixing bowl. Beat 1 minute. Add powdered sugar and beat another minute. Add the pudding mix and cocoa; beat until firm. Fold in 1½ cups whipped topping and pour into crust. Chill until very firm. Top with remaining whipped topping and garnish with shaved chocolate.

Yields 8 servings

The O'Malley Farm Cafe—Fine Family Dining Since 1976
403 West Main Street
Waunakee, Wisconsin 53597
608-849-7401

Open April 1 to October 31

Monday and Tuesday 6:00 a.m. to 2:00 p.m.
Wednesday, Thursday, Saturday, and Sunday
6:00 a.m. to 8:00 p.m.
Friday 6:00 a.m. to 9:00 a.m.

November 1 to March 31

Monday through Thursday 6:00 a.m. to 2:00 p.m.
Friday 6:00 a.m. to 9:00 p.m.
Saturday and Sunday 6:00 a.m. to 8:00 p.m.

MasterCard and Visa accepted

O'Malley's, a gathering place for their local clientele, also draws guests from the surrounding area as it boasts to be "only ten minutes from anywhere"! They offer a full menu and are famous for such breakfast specialties as their incredible cinnamon rolls. The Cafe has also become known for its excellent soups. The "soup sampler" is filled with the soup of the day and everyone is invited to sample the soup, regardless of what they may order.

The casual atmosphere of the Cafe is demonstrated by the expansion of the counter seating concept to an "open seating" table where guests may seat themselves and enjoy a meal or a cup of coffee and not dine alone.

In the privacy of the sunny, tastefully decorated banquet rooms, the atmosphere of the Cafe can be changed from family-oriented dining to a romantic anniversary dinner to a business meeting without interruptions. Overall, the O'Malley's stress hospitality.

IRISH BROWN BREAD

This recipe was brought from Ireland by Martha (O'Malley) Scanlon. It's a must for all St. Patrick's Day celebrations.

3/4	cup wheat germ
1 1/2	cups white flour
1 1/2	cups wheat flour
2	tablespoons sugar
1	teaspoon salt
1	teaspoon baking soda
2 1/2	cups Wisconsin buttermilk

Preheat oven to 350 degrees. Mix dry ingredients together. Add buttermilk gradually to make a moist dough. Pour into greased and floured 12-inch pie tin.

Bake for approximately 1 hour 15 minutes. Insert knife into center of loaf. Bread is done when knife comes out clean. Cool. Cut into 12 equal triangles. Serve warm or at room temperature with butter.

Yields 12 servings

The Oaks Dining & Spirits
E12603 Kilpatrick Point Drive #4
Merrimac, Wisconsin 53561
608-643-6723

Memorial Day through Labor Day
open daily 4:00 p.m. to 9:00 p.m.

Winter hours
Wednesday through Sunday 4:00 p.m. to 9:00 p.m.

Year-round Sunday brunch 10:00 a.m. to 2:00 p.m.

All major credit cards accepted

The view overlooking Lake Wisconsin provides the perfect setting for a relaxed evening of fine dining.

Take a ferry ride to Merrimac—we're only minutes away off Highway 78 before Prairie du Sac, or enjoy a ride through the picturesque countryside. Summer boat docking is available. We are also located on the snowmobile trail.

Our menu includes local favorites and gourmet dining at affordable prices. Weekends include Friday night fish fry and Saturday Prime Rib. Our Sunday brunch features smoked salmon, fresh fruits, cheeses, full salad bar, hot entrees, waffles, and chef-made-to-order omelettes in the dining room. We feature a wide array of appetizers, salads, pastas, steaks, seafood, and wild game.

Get away from it all on our deck with its panoramic view of beautiful Lake Wisconsin, or in the winter, enjoy the warmth of our fieldstone fireplace.

TENDERLOIN OF PORK "FLORENTINE"

This is a great alternative to beef or chicken, although either can be used as a substitute for the pork. To decrease the fat and calories in this dish, broil the meat, eliminating the breading.

A wine which complements the sauce very well is 1991 Lindeman's "Bin 65," an Australian chardonnay. Or choose your favorite chardonnay or Sauvignon Blanc.

Sauce St. Germain:
- ¼ pound bacon, raw and julienne
- ½ cup julienne onion
- ½ cup sugar
- ½ cup vinegar
- 2 tablespoons cornstarch
- ½ cup water
- 1 tablespoon parsley, chopped

- 2 cups fresh spinach, washed, deveined and patted dry*
- 1½ pounds pork tenderloin, silver skin removed
- Salt and pepper to taste
- 2 cups sifted flour
- 2 eggs, whipped
- 2 cups cracker meal, crushed fine
- ½ cup salad oil or bacon fat
- 1 hard boiled egg, chopped fine

In medium saucepan, fry bacon until crisp; drain off excess grease. Add onions to bacon and saute until tender and transparent. Add sugar and caramelize until golden brown. Add vinegar and bring to a boil. Mix cornstarch with water and dissolve. Add mixture to boiling saucepan and whisk to blend. Return to boil; reduce heat and simmer 15 minutes. Add parsley; stir to blend and reduce heat to low, holding until service.

Heat deep-fat fryer or Fry Daddy to 350 degrees. (If not available, use a deep kettle with 1-1½ inches salad oil.) Place spinach leaves into basket and lower into oil. Cook until bubbling stops, about 1-1½ minutes.* Remove spinach from oil and let basket hang to allow all oil to drain away; set aside.

Trim pork loin and cut into 12 cutlets. Pound cutlets flat with side of knife or kitchen mallet. Sprinkle with salt and pepper. Make a simple breading station with three bowls; one with flour; the second with egg; and the third with cracker meal. Dust cutlet in flour, patting off excess. Dip in egg and coat evenly. Roll in cracker meal and press to adhere crumbs. Let stand 5 minutes for crust to set.

In 12-inch skillet or electric fry pan, place salad oil or bacon fat and heat to about 300-325 degrees. Fry cutlet until golden brown on each side. Place browned cutlets on paper towel to absorb excess oil. To serve, place prepared spinach in center of each plate. Place 3 cutlets on each bed of spinach. Top each cutlet with equal amount of sauce. Top with chopped egg for garnish and decorate plate with radish flowers or fresh flower garnish.

*It is imperative to use fresh, dry spinach leaves—not frozen or wet to prevent fire or boil-over of your fryer.

Yields 4 servings

Old Town Pub
724 South Gammon Road
Madison, Wisconsin 53719
608-276-8589

Open Sunday through Thursday
11:00 a.m. to 2:00 p.m.

Friday and Saturday
11:00 a.m. to 2:30 p.m.

If you're looking for a spot that serves great burgers and excellent reuben sandwiches, and may remind you just a bit of "the bar where everybody knows your name," then the Old Town Pub should be your choice.

Since March of 1990, Old Town Pub has been serving up homemade soups, chili, and salads on Madison's west side. In addition, Old Town features soup and sandwich specials, Friday lunch fish fry, and shrimp basket. Stop in any weekday, Monday through Friday from 3:00 p.m. to 6:00 p.m. and enjoy Happy Hour with reduced drink prices and delicious munchies.

There's lots to do at this neighborhood pub. Choose from darts or pinball if you're into participatory sports, or relax in front of the satellite T.V. for great sports action. Call ahead and carry out if you'd like to enjoy Old Town's food right at home.

Old Town Pub is locally owned and operated by Harry and Laura Hollman.

OLD TOWN PUB COLESLAW

We developed this recipe after our customers told us our coleslaw could use more flavor. I hope you enjoy this tasty salad.

4	cups packed, raw shredded cabbage, chilled
1/2	cup packed, raw grated carrots, chilled
1/4	teaspoon garlic powder
1/2	teaspoon white pepper
1	teaspoon seasoned salt
3/4-1	cup coleslaw dressing (onion seed salad dressing), chilled

Mix cabbage and carrots thoroughly with spices. Add 3/4 cup dressing and mix well. Chill coleslaw; as it chills, cabbage will lose some of its water, adding more liquid to the dressing. Before serving, add remaining 1/4 cup dressing if desired.

Yields 4-6 servings

MILWAUKEE'S PREFERRED HOTEL

**The Pfister Hotel
424 East Wisconsin Avenue
Milwaukee, Wisconsin 53202
414-273-8222**

*Open lunch Monday through Friday
11:30 a.m. to 2:00 p.m.*

*Dinner Monday through Friday and Sunday
5:30 p.m. to 10:00 p.m.*

Saturday 5:30 p.m. to 11:00 p.m.

All major credit cards accepted

For an incomparable dining experience, the award-winning English Room provides a select array of delicious cuisine, from traditional favorites to flavorful and creative dishes.

REGAL PLUM PUDDING

*This recipe has been a tradition in The English Room
of The Pfister Hotel for many years.*

1	1-pound loaf raisin bread
2^1/$_3$	cups Wisconsin whole milk
12	ounces beef suet, ground
1^1/$_3$	cups brown sugar, packed
2^3/$_4$	cups beaten eggs
^{1}/$_3$	cup orange juice
1^1/$_3$	teaspoons vanilla
2^3/$_4$	cups raisins
1^1/$_3$	cups chopped dates
2	cups diced candied fruit
^{1}/$_3$	teaspoon orange peel
^{3}/$_4$	cup chopped walnuts
1^1/$_3$	cups all-purpose flour
2^3/$_4$	teaspoons ground cinnamon
1^1/$_3$	teaspoons ground cloves
1^1/$_3$	teaspoons ground mace
1^1/$_3$	teaspoons baking soda
^{3}/$_4$	teaspoon salt

Soak bread in milk and beat to break up. Stir in ground suet, brown sugar, eggs, orange juice and vanilla. In a separate bowl, combine raisins, dates, candied fruits, orange peel, and nuts. In another bowl, stir together flour, cinnamon, cloves, mace, soda, and salt; add to mixed fruit and mix well. Stir in bread/suet mixture. Pour into well greased 2-quart mold. Cover with foil and tie on tightly. Place mold in pan with boiling water and cover. Steam for 3^1/$_2$ hours. Add more boiling water if needed.

Yields 10-12 servings

The Pine Baron's
149 County W
PO Box 458
Manitowish Waters, Wisconsin 54545
715-543-8464

Open Thursday-Tuesday

Lunch from 11:00 a.m.

Dinner from 5:00 p.m.

Late-night fare from 9:00 p.m.

Discover, MasterCard, Visa accepted

The Pine Baron's was established in 1993 by Mary and Henry Sinkus, who left the corporate world to fulfill their dream of owning a small business in the northwoods of Wisconsin. Henry had previously owned culinary equipment stores, catered and taught gourmet cooking. When Mary, who had vacationed in Manitowish Waters for over 30 years, introduced him to the area six years ago, the decision to make their move was a natural.

The Pine Baron's offers intimate dining in a casual country setting. All menu items, from unique appetizers to gourmet desserts, are prepared to order using only the freshest ingredients. To enhance your dining experience, espresso and cappuccino are offered as well as the unique tastes of a carefully chosen selection of fine wine, micro-brewed and imported beers and the finest in spirits. Exceptional food together with the relaxing atmosphere of unique antiques and a collection of local memorabilia create a delightful combination of the elegant and the casual.

The dinner menu features farm-raised wild game (Pork Chop stuffed with Pheasant Sausage or Venison Wellington, for example), Roast Duckling with Raspberry Sauce, Baby-Back Ribs prepared with the Chef's prize-winning barbecue sauce, Cioppino (seafood stew), Mussels Marinara, Boeuf Wellington and a wonderful selection of steaks, chops, veal, chicken, seafood and fresh pasta. For lunch you will find Caesar Salad, Eggs Benedict and a varied selection of sandwiches (including the Chef's famous Italian Beef and Philadelphia Cheese Steak) and tantalizing homemade soups.

MOUSSE OF WALLEYE AND SHRIMP

*The Mousse of Walleye and Shrimp, created in our own kitchen,
is a selection from our catering menu as well as an appetizer
in the restaurant. This distinctive item is a wonderful hors d'oeuvres
or first course (served with a horseradish hollandaise sauce and caviar)
to begin a gourmet meal or an exquisite accompaniment
(served on toast points or pumpernickel rye bread) at a cocktail party.*

1 28-ounce skinned walleye filet	1/2 teaspoon onion powder
11 ounces peeled and deveined shrimp	1/2 teaspoon garlic powder
1/4 cup shelled, roasted pistachios	1/2 teaspoon ground oregano
1 1/2 teaspoons celery salt	1/2 teaspoon black pepper
1 teaspoon white pepper	3 tablespoons sherry
1/2 teaspoon sweet paprika	1 cup heavy Wisconsin whipping cream

Preheat oven to 400 degrees. Lightly butter an 11 x 4-inch pate terrine and the cover. Cut a piece of parchment or waxed paper to line the inside of the cover and butter the paper.

Place walleye filet in food processor bowl fitted with knife blade. Process until coarsely chopped, about 20 seconds. Add shrimp and process for an additional 20 seconds. Add pistachios and process for approximately 10 seconds more until well blended. Add celery salt, white pepper, paprika, onion powder, garlic powder, oregano, black pepper and sherry. Process for approximately 10 seconds until well blended. With food processor on, slowly add cream and process until the mixture is amalgamated into a smooth paste, approximately 30 seconds.

Spoon mixture into the buttered pate terrine, packing well and smoothing the top with a spoon or spatula. Cover the top with the parchment paper and place the lid on the terrine. Place terrine in a deep baking pan. Fill pan with water to 2/3 the height of the terrine. Place in 400-degree oven and bake for 40 minutes or until internal temperature of mousse is 180 degrees. Remove from water bath to cooling rack—carefully remove lid and parchment paper. When cool, unmold mousse, wrap in plastic wrap and refrigerate for at least 1 hour, preferably overnight.

For serving, slice 1/4-inch thick with an electric knife.

Yields 4-6 servings

Polecat & Lace

Polecat & Lace

427 Oneida Avenue

PO Box 601

Minocqua, Wisconsin 54548

715-356-3335

Open Monday through Saturday from 11:00 a.m.

MasterCard and Visa accepted

As you're traveling northern Wisconsin for the fishing, the hunting, the snowmobiling, the summer activities, or the relaxation, be sure to stop by Polecat & Lace in Minocqua. Whether you're a summer traveler dropping in for a piece of homemade dessert and a cool drink or a winter outdoor enthusiast in to warm up with a bowl of homemade soup, you'll feel welcome at Polecat & Lace.

Where does the name come from? The menu at Polecat & Lace opens with the answer to a question that must have been asked many times by out-of-town guests.

"Polecat" is the term lumberjacks used to refer to skunks; later, it was used to refer to the lumberjacks themselves, whose odor was probably not unlike that of a skunk when they came in from the woods. The rugged loggers were also known for their hearty appetites. Lace is representative of all things refined and civilized—the very antithesis of a lumberjack.

When the restaurant was built, the owners wanted its name to reflect the timber heritage of the region as well as a sensibility to fine food and elegant dining. Thus, the menu offers food hearty enough for a hungry "polecat," served in an atmosphere that would not be unsuitable for a turn-of-the century lady in lacy finery.

The Pitzo family, Joan, Michael, and Denise, own and operate the restaurant and pub. The warmth of beautiful oak, casual atmosphere, and friendly staff make it a relaxed place for you to spend your days of leisure.

CRAB CAKE APPETIZERS

These crab cakes are simple to prepare and are very tasty.
They work well as a first course to a meal or are great with cocktails.

2	ounces uncooked angel hair pasta
6	ounces crabmeat, well drained
2	tablespoons minced celery
2	tablespoons minced green onion
1	tablespoon minced green pepper
1	teaspoon Worcestershire sauce
$^1/_2$	cup bread crumbs
2	tablespoons Miracle Whip
1	egg
	Vegetable oil for frying
2	lemons, garnish

Break uncooked pasta into 1-1$^1/_2$-inch lengths. Cook, drain well, and cool. Combine next 7 ingredients in medium-size bowl. Beat egg well and add to mixture. Add cooled pasta, mix well, and refrigerate 2 hours or overnight.

Pour oil in deep fryer or place $^3/_4$-inch oil in heavy skillet; heat oil to 350 degrees. Form mixture into small mounds and flatten to $^3/_4$-inch thick cakes or form into small balls. Deep fry 3-4 minutes or until golden brown and crisp. Keep warm in 200-degree oven until serving. Cut lemons into wedges and use as garnish.

Yields 12-14 appetizer servings

Ristorante Brissago
Grand Geneva Resort & Spa
7036 Grand Way
Lake Geneva, Wisconsin 53147
414-248-8811

Open Sunday and Tuesday through Thursday
5:30 p.m. to 9:00 p.m.

Friday and Saturday 5:30 p.m. to 10:00 p.m.

All major credit cards accepted

The soaring Alps form a majestic background for the historic village of Brissago in the lake district of northern Italy. Located on beautiful Lake Maggiore, Brissago is as famous for its hospitality as its spectacular scenery. The village has for centuries been a favorite resting place for travelers crossing the border between Italy and Switzerland. Ristorante Brissago is named for this town because the Italian-Swiss lake country is so similar to the Lake Geneva area. The restaurant features traditional Italian cuisine augmented with regional specialties and contemporary Italian creations, along with an extensive wine list.

PENNE ROBERTO

*Penne Roberto is Chef Fedorko's favorite recipe because
it is simple, light, fresh and easy to prepare at home.*

1	large yellow onion, finely diced
4	large tablespoons chopped garlic
6	tablespoons extra virgin olive oil, divided
12	Roma tomatoes, peeled and roughly chopped
1/2	cup chopped, fresh basil or 4 tablespoons dry basil, divided
	Salt and freshly ground pepper to taste
6	ounces pancetta (Italian bacon) or any good quality bacon
10	ounces dry Penne pasta
4	ounces Wisconsin Parmesan cheese, grated

Sweat onions and garlic in 4 tablespoons oil to flavor oil. When onions are translucent, add tomatoes and a little over 1/2 of the basil. Cook approximately 20 minutes and season with salt and freshly ground pepper.

Cook bacon until crisp and all fat is rendered; drain. Cook pasta in large amount of boiling, salted water until al dente; chill under cold, running water to stop cooking process.

When you're ready to serve, run pasta under hot water to heat; allow to drain. In large serving bowl, mix remaining oil and basil, toss with pasta, and season with salt and pepper. Top with tomato sauce, bacon, and freshly grated Parmesan cheese.

Yields 4 servings

Rock Garden Supper Club
1951 Bond Street
Green Bay, Wisconsin 54303
414-497-4701

*Open lunch Monday through Friday
11:00 a.m. to 2:00 p.m.*

*Dinner Monday through Friday
5:00 p.m. to 10:00 p.m.*

Saturday 5:00 p.m. to 11:00 p.m.

*Sunday Brunch 10:00 a.m. to 2:00 p.m.,
dinner 4:00 p.m. to 9:00 p.m.*

All major credit cards accepted

The Rock Garden has been a family business since 1978. We currently have 140 seats in our dining room which serves luncheons daily and a varied menu seven days a week. Our banquet rooms have seating for 1000 people in various rooms.

POTATO SOUP

This potato soup is featured on our Polish-American buffet
which is served every Thursday night.
It has been a local favorite for many years.

1	cup Wisconsin butter
1/2	cup diced celery
1/2	cup diced onion
4	cups Wisconsin heavy cream
1	8- to 10-ounce can chicken stock
1	cup diced red potatoes
	Salt and pepper to taste
1/4	cup chopped parsley

In a medium saute pan, melt butter over medium heat; add celery and onions. Saute until tender, 5-8 minutes. Add heavy cream and reduce by one half. In a medium saucepan, place chicken stock and potatoes and bring to a boil. Cook until potatoes are tender, approximately 10 minutes. Combine all ingredients in saucepan and stir until fully blended. Salt and pepper to taste. Garnish with chopped parsley.

Yields 4-6 servings

a restaurant

The Sandhill Inn
170 East Main Street
PO Box 85
Merrimac, Wisconsin 53561
608-493-2203

Open Tuesday through Saturday 5:30 p.m. to 10:00 p.m.

Sunday brunch 9:30 a.m. to 2:00 p.m.

American Express, MasterCard and Visa accepted

The Sandhill Inn is located in scenic Merrimac, Wisconsin, home of the famous free ferry. The Sandhill Inn was opened in 1989 to showcase Wisconsin's finest products. We feature lamb, veal and, of course, beef. Another favorite dish is Atlantic salmon. Chef Paul makes almost everything from scratch except the wine and beer which we import from Middleton (Garten Brau) and Prairie du Sac (Wollersheim Wine). The tables are appointed with fresh flowers and linen tablecloths.

The Sandhill Inn sits in an old Victorian-style home, built around 1896 by John Rotzall, the area blacksmith. The inside of the restaurant is lined with beautiful oak trim and a winding staircase, while the outside is rather plain. The rumor is Mr. Rotzall did it that way so the people in the village did not know how much money he was making. The home, with three stories above the ground and a basement, was built for $1,000.00.

From the spring to fall, the outside is blessed with the past ladies' hard work in the garden. There are jack-in-the-pulpits, shooting stars, fiddle heads, cap lilies, surprise lilies (Naked Ladies), New England asters, and brilliant fall trees. The saying goes when you plant something it's not for you, it's for someone else, and we are thoroughly enjoying the beauty of their work.

The original blacksmith shop is next door to the restaurant. Steve Hackbarth is the current blacksmith. His work is as creative as The Sandhill Inn's food. Recently he made an elaborate chandelier for a home in Chicago. His work can be viewed six days a week.

BEEF TOURNEDOS WITH MUSHROOM DUXELLE

This item is the most popular at The Sandhill Inn.
The Mushroom Duxelle is very similar to pate and goes well
with the beef but with other meats too.

¹/₂	teaspoon salt
¹/₂	teaspoon paprika
¹/₂	teaspoon ground white pepper
4	5-ounce beef tenderloins
¹/₂	cup olive oil
1	8-ounce package button mushrooms
4	slices bacon, chopped
1	teaspoon chopped garlic
1¹/₂	cups Wisconsin heavy whipping cream
1	cup bread crumbs, approximately

Combine salt, paprika, and ground white pepper. Sprinkle mixture on both sides of tenderloins. Pour olive oil into large saute pan. Heat olive oil on medium heat. Place tenderloins in heated oil. Brown both sides of tenderloin. Set tenderloins aside.

In a large saucepot, place mushrooms, bacon, chopped garlic, and heavy whipping cream. Reduce mixture by half over medium heat. Remember to stir mushroom mixture while cooking to prevent scalding pot. Remove reduced mushroom mixture from pot and place in blender and puree. Place puree mixture in large bowl and stir in bread crumbs until mixture is dry. This mixture will look like a dry paste when the bread crumbs are completely incorporated. Place this mixture in a pastry bag with a star tip and pipe mushroom duxelle mixture onto the seared beef tenderloins.

Bake in preheated oven at 400 degrees to desired cooking temperature, 5-10 minutes. You may finish this dish with one of your favorite sauces over the top of the tenderloins. Here at The Sandhill Inn, we use veal demi-glaze. There are a number of instant-style sauces out on the market today that would make it easy to prepare at home.

Yields 4 servings

Tailgate Restaurant & Motel
14075 Highway 32/64
PO Box 68
Mountain, Wisconsin 54149
715-276-7200

Open daily, serving from 6:00 a.m.

Closed Christmas Day

The Tailgate Restaurant & Motel is located on the edge of the Nicolet Forest in the town of Mountain.

Over the past 18 years, the Tailgate has developed a reputation for super home-cooked meals prepared under the watchful eyes of Ron and Lill Heuser. Whether it's a stop for breakfast, lunch, dinner or a snack, the "daily specials" are prepared and served by the Tailgate staff with fresh and wholesome ingredients and plenty of love.

The restaurant is open daily at 6:00 a.m. and serves a complete menu including steaks, chops, seafood and a bountiful soup and salad bar in the summer and fall (May to December).

People enjoy the food. Top off your meal with our "deep dish" apple pie with cinnamon ice cream, whipped cream and cinnamon sugar topping or try a few of Lillian's homemade cookies served daily. (The Tailgate makes and sells about 1/2 ton of Christmas cookies every Christmas season!)

TAILGATE PISTACHIO DESSERT

Simple, fast and delicious!
This is also good as a pie filling served well-chilled
in a baked graham cracker or cookie crumb crust.

1	20-ounce can Dole crushed pineapple in unsweetened juice (do not drain)
1	5-ounce package Jello brand instant pistachio pudding mix (added dry)
$1/2$	of $10^1/2$-ounce bag miniature marshmallows
1	8-ounce carton Cool Whip whipped topping
$1/2$	cup shredded coconut

In mixing bowl with electric mixer, combine first 4 ingredients in order listed, mixing well after each addition. Fold in coconut. Cover and refrigerate overnight. Serve in a pretty parfait glass if desired.

If desired, add any of the following variations after combining first 4 ingredients: $1/2$ to $3/4$ cup well drained red maraschino cherries (Christmas); $1/2$ to $3/4$ cup seedless red or green grapes (whole); 6 ounces well drained mandarin orange sections; $1/4$ cup slivered almonds or chopped pecans.

Yields 8 servings

RON'S CELERY SEED COLESLAW DRESSING

Try this tasty dressing on chicken salad or fruit salad too.

$1^1/2$	cups white sugar	3	cups vegetable oil
$1/2$	tablespoon salt	$1/2$	cup white vinegar
1	tablespoon horseradish mustard	$2^1/4$	teaspoons whole celery seed
$1/4$	cup grated onion		

Combine sugar, salt, mustard, and onion in a mixing bowl. Add a small amount of oil in a thin stream; mix with electric mixer. Add a small amount of vinegar in a thin stream and mix well. Alternate adding remaining oil and vinegar, ending with oil. When thoroughly mixed, add celery seed.

Yields approximately 4 cups

Third Street Pier
1110 Old World Third Street
Milwaukee, Wisconsin 53203
414-272-0330

Open daily lunch 11:30 a.m. to 2:00 p.m.

Dinner 5:00 p.m. to 10:00 p.m.

All major credit cards accepted

Our stunning, romantic restaurant offers the finest in seafood and steak with a great view of the river and city skyline. Seafood specialties include Caribbean Bouillabaisse, Dover Sole, Shrimp Provencal, Seafood Linguine, Grilled Swordfish, Orange Roughy, Cajun Catfish, Crab Legs, and Lobster Tail. Steaks include New York Strip, Filet Mignon, Beef Tournedos Florentine, and Grilled Prime Rib of Beef. Our award-winning wine list is sure to enhance your dining experience.

Enjoy unique appetizers, homemade desserts and Friday fish fry with potato pancakes. Beautiful party facilities are available.

CARIBBEAN BOUILLABAISSE

Prep time is a bit long but actual cooking time is not. Bouillabaisse is an extremely tasty dish, loaded with seafood and vegetables. It is low in fat but full of flavor. Bouillabaisse originated along the harbors of France. Our Caribbean version adds a touch of spice.

1 cup chopped carrots, 1-inch pieces	1 teaspoon dried marjoram
2 stalks celery, chopped	1 teaspoon dried basil
1 cup chopped onions, 1-inch pieces	2 6-8-ounce lobster tails,
2 tablespoons olive oil	thawed if frozen and split length-wise
4 cloves garlic, chopped	1 8-ounce swordfish filet, cut into 4 pieces
1 cup chopped tomatoes, 1-inch pieces	4 Cherrystone clams, scrubbed
1 cup chopped potatoes, 1-inch pieces	12 mussels, scrubbed and beard removed
1/4 teaspoon saffron	12 jumbo shrimp, peeled and deveined
4 cups clam juice	8 Littleneck clams, scrubbed
2/3 cup tomato juice	12 1/2 ounces sea scallops
1 cup dry white wine	4 king crab legs, split
3 cups water	Salt and pepper to taste
1 dash Tabasco sauce	1 tablespoon chopped parsley
1/2 teaspoon dried thyme	1 bunch green onions

*All mollusks that are not closed before cooking should be discarded.

In 4-quart saucepan, saute carrots, celery and onions in olive oil until onions are translucent. Add garlic, tomato, potato, and saffron. Cook over low heat 1 minute. Add clam juice, tomato juice, wine, water, Tabasco, and remaining herbs. Turn heat to high and bring to a boil. Boil 4 minutes.

Add lobster, cover and cook 2 minutes. Add swordfish and Cherrystone clams. Cover and cook for a few minutes. Add mussels, shrimp, Littleneck clams, scallops, and crab legs. Cover pot and cook 4 minutes. At this point, all mollusks should be opened and the lobster cooked through. If not, continue cooking 2 more minutes.

Remove from heat. Divide fish and seafood into 4 large bowls. Salt and pepper broth to taste. Ladle broth and vegetables into each bowl. Garnish with chopped parsley and green onion.

Serve with slices of Italian bread seasoned with olive oil and Wisconsin Parmesan cheese, then baked.

Yields 4 servings

Vern's Dorf Haus
8931 Highway Y
Sauk City, Wisconsin 53583
608-643-3980

Open Wednesday and Thursday 5:00 p.m. to 9:00 p.m.

Friday and Saturday 5:00 p.m. to 10:30 p.m.

Sunday 11:30 a.m. to 8:30 p.m.

Bavarian Smorgasbord—first Monday of each month
5:00 p.m. to 9:00 p.m.

MasterCard and Visa accepted

Nestled in the small German village of Roxbury, an old world atmosphere awaits you at Vern's Dorf Haus. Decorated with authentic antiques, paintings of famous German castles and Kings, and breathtaking stained glass, the Dorf Haus will enchant you.

Our extensive menu offers a variety of authentic German and American specialties that will satisfy the most discriminating palate. From wiener schnitzel, sauerbraten, rouladen, and pork shank to prime rib, bar-b-que ribs, duck, and our famous family-style chicken, you will find only the best meats and freshest ingredients are used in preparing your entree. From a menu which was begun over 35 years ago and comprised of only family-style chicken and fish to today's extensive menu, the Maier's have not forgotten what good food and service are built on.

Located 20 miles northwest of Madison, 3 miles southeast of Sauk City and central to many Wisconsin attractions, your visit to the Dorf Haus will be enjoyable and convenient. St. Norbert's Church, the oldest Catholic church in Dane and Sauk counties, is located across the street. The paintings and beautiful art glass in the windows are well worth a visit.

ROULADEN

This Dorf Haus specialty is easy to prepare and freezes well!

4   slices beef top round, $^1/_2$-inch thick
    Salt and pepper
4   tablespoons prepared mustard
3   onions, finely chopped
3   slices bacon, chopped
1   pickle, sliced
1   tablespoon vegetable shortening
1   generous cup meat stock
1   tablespoon all-purpose flour
$^1/_4$ cup dry white wine
1   2-ounce can sliced mushrooms, drained

Season beef with salt and pepper; spread 1 tablespoon mustard thinly over each slice. Sprinkle $^2/_3$ of onion, bacon, and pickle over beef. Roll up slices and secure with skewers. Heat shortening in medium skillet and add beef rolls. Saute until well browned, turning occasionally. Add remaining onion; saute until light golden brown. Add meat stock. Season to taste with salt and pepper. Cover and simmer about 1 hour.

To thicken sauce, combine flour, wine, and sliced mushrooms. Stir flour mixture into cooking liquid. Cook and stir until slightly thickened. Remove skewers and serve rouladen.

Yields 4 servings

The **Village Inn**

Food Spirits and Lodging

The Village Inn
Junction Highway 13 & County Road C
PO Box 127
Cornucopia, Wisconsin 54827
715-742-3941

Open Memorial Day to second week of October
Monday through Thursday 5:00 p.m. to 9:00 p.m.
Friday and Saturday 5:00 p.m. to 10:00 p.m.
Sunday 12:00 p.m. to 9:00 p.m.

Second week of October through Memorial Day
Friday and Saturday 5:00 p.m. to 9:00 p.m.
Sunday 12:00 p.m. to 6:00 p.m.

MasterCard and Visa accepted

A pleasant surprise awaits you when visiting The Village Inn on the south shore of Lake Superior in the peaceful town of Cornucopia. The ambience of a true country inn welcomes guests as a perfect place for a relaxed, romantic get-a-way. First you might like to stop into the friendly tavern for a hearty lunch and your favorite beverage before checking into one of the four guest rooms.

In the evening, you will enjoy dinner in the gracious country restaurant with its charming decor. Whether a romantic dinner for two, family gathering or special occasion party, The Village Inn is most accommodating with its friendly, courteous staff and varied menu. Fresh Lake Superior whitefish or trout are specialties as well as the homemade fish chowder. A thoughtful "lighter fare" is provided for the smaller appetite.

In summer, arrange to be a part of "The Village Inn's Fish Boil," a fun activity, centered around an open fire with a simmering kettle of fish, potatoes, and onions. The event is served in the outdoor pavilion which makes this a very casual and entertaining evening.

Owners Ruth and George Grubbe want your stay to be a memorable one. With weekend specials such as Friday fish fry and Cook's Choice Sunday dinner, you'll want to make The Village Inn a tradition of your northern Wisconsin travels. That's why The Village Inn is called "a good place to come back to."

THE ORIGINAL CHICKEN A LA KING

You'll find many a version of this recipe, but none can match the original for luscious flavor and delicate consistency. In the early 1960s, women's clubs thrived on it, hostesses swore by it and brides were launched with Chicken a la King...

1/4 cup chopped green pepper	3 egg yolks
1 cup thinly sliced mushrooms	1/2 teaspoon paprika
1/4 cup plus 2 tablespoons Wisconsin butter	1 teaspoon fresh onion juice
2 tablespoons enriched flour	1 tablespoon fresh lemon juice
3/4 teaspoon salt	2 tablespoons cooking sherry
2 cups Wisconsin light cream	1/4 cup diced pimiento
3 cups cooked chicken, cut in pieces	

Cook green pepper and mushrooms in 2 tablespoons of butter until tender but not brown; push vegetables to one side and blend flour and salt into the butter. Gradually stir in cream; cook and stir until sauce thickens. Add chicken, and heat thoroughly, stirring occasionally.

Meanwhile, in a small bowl, blend egg yolks, paprika, and remaining butter, softened; set aside. To chicken mixture add onion juice, lemon juice, and sherry. Heat chicken to bubbling then add egg yolk mixture all at once, stirring until blended. Immediately remove from heat. Add pimiento. Serve at once in Cheese Toast Cups.

CHEESE TOAST CUPS

1 1-pound unsliced sandwich loaf	1/2 cup light cream
1/3 cup Wisconsin butter, melted	2 cups shredded Wisconsin sharp
1 egg, beaten	process American cheese

Freeze loaf for easy handling. Trim crusts from unsliced loaf; cut in 8 thick slices. Place each slice flat on a surface. On the side of each slice of bread, cut a slit parallel to the surface 1/2 inch from the bottom, extending the slit to within 1/2 inch of each corner. Make a slit like this on each of the 4 sides of the slice. From above the bread, cut down 1/2 inch from sides of the slice to the slits, making a square. Lift out this inner square and discard.

Place bread cups on ungreased baking sheet; brush with butter inside and out. Combine egg, cream, and cheese; fill cups 1/2 full. Bake in 350-degree oven 15-20 minutes, until golden brown and custard is set. Fill with Chicken a la King.

Yields 8 servings

Wayne's Family Restaurant
805 Brazeau Avenue
Highway 41 North
Oconto, Wisconsin 54153
414-834-4262

Open Sunday 6:00 a.m. to 10:00 p.m.

Monday through Saturday 5:00 a.m. to 10:00 p.m.

MasterCard and Visa accepted

Whether you're heading north or south, Wayne's Family Restaurant offers a full-service family dining experience.

We feature as many as four kinds of homemade soups daily, with chicken dumpling being our specialty. We also offer the largest variety of baked-from-scratch pies north of Green Bay. Try our fresh-cut apple and Dutch apple pies, and for those who cannot have sugar, we now feature sugar-free home-baked apple, wild berry, and cherry pies.

We also have daily breakfast and dinner specials plus our full menu. Sunday morning, 8:00 a.m. to 11:00 a.m., try our delicious breakfast buffet and mouth-watering dessert bar featuring a great variety of delectable fruits and desserts. And on Friday nights enjoy the all-you-can-eat fish buffet and salad bar or choose from five other fish or dinner specials.

Browse among our many fine gifts for something special for that certain someone, or take along a gift certificate so someone else may enjoy a visit.

We are also at your service for catering, weddings, company parties, picnics, anniversaries, birthdays—anything special that you may be celebrating.

Wayne and Karen Bostwick, together with their employees, would like to extend a warm welcome to you. Whether you live in the area or are just passing through, enjoy our friendly atmosphere, home-cooking, mouth-watering aromas, and happy, smiling waitresses. We truly want to make your visit an enjoyable one!

RICE PUDDING

A delicious addition to any meal or as a dessert served with whipped cream. Low-fat and sugar-free substitutes can be used.

8	cups Wisconsin milk (for low-fat use skim)
5	eggs
1¹/₂	cups sugar (for low-fat use ¹/₂ cup Equal)
³/₄	cups cornstarch
	Dash of salt
2	teaspoons vanilla
4	cups cooked rice
2	cups cooked raisins
	Sprinkle of cinnamon

In 3-quart saucepan, bring milk just to a boil. In the meantime, blend eggs, sugar, and cornstarch. When milk starts to boil, remove from heat immediately and add mixture to milk together with salt and vanilla. Mix just a few minutes, until pudding starts to thicken. Stir in cooked rice and raisins. Pour into large serving bowl and sprinkle with cinnamon. Serve warm or chilled.

Yields 8-10 servings

Wendt's on the Lake

Established 1961

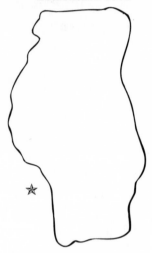

Wendt's on the Lake
N9699 Lakeshore Drive
Van Dyne, Wisconsin 54979
414-688-5231

*Open Monday through Thursday and Saturday
11:00 a.m. to 10:00 p.m.*

Friday 11:00 a.m. to 11:00 p.m.

Sunday 11:00 a.m. to 9:00 p.m.

Wendt's on the Lake, overlooking beautiful Lake Winnebago, has been recognized for its fish fries, prime rib, and deep-fried lobster. It has won industry awards for each of these items. "Our perch, fresh from Canadian lakes, is known all over," says owner, Linda Wendt. On a typical Friday evening, Wendt's serves approximately 600-700 meals. Enjoy an outdoor lunch or dinner on picnic tables during the summer months.

SIRLOIN TIPS

2	pounds sirloin tip, cut in $1/2$-inch cubes
2	tablespoons Wisconsin butter
$1/2$	cup finely diced celery
$1/2$	cup finely diced onion
	Water, enough to cover meat
$1^1/2$	tablespoons beef base
8	ounces sliced, fresh mushrooms
1	tablespoon Kitchen Bouquet (brown sauce)
$1/2$	tablespoon garlic powder
$1/4$	teaspoon ground basil
$1/8$	teaspoon ground thyme
$1/8$	teaspoon ground oregano
$1/2$	cup flour

In a large skillet, brown meat in butter until partially cooked, 20-30 minutes. Add celery, onions, water, beef base, and mushrooms. Cook an additional 10-15 minutes. Add Kitchen Bouquet and spices. Thicken sauce with paste of flour and $1/2$ cup water. Simmer 1 hour or until meat is tender. Serve over buttered noodles.

Yields 6 servings

The Wilson Street Grill
217 South Hamilton Street
Madison, Wisconsin 53703
608-251-3500

Open Monday through Friday,

Lunch 11:00 a.m. to 2:00 p.m.

Open Monday through Saturday

Dinner 5:30 p.m. to 9:30 p.m.

MasterCard and Visa accepted

A block and a half southwest of the Capitol Square, The Wilson Street Grill, a Christy & Craig Associates Restaurant, is noted for its contemporary cooking, its permanent collection of Tandem Press fine art prints, fresh flowers, excellent American wines and local beers. The "grill" is used creatively with fresh fish, chicken and quail, seafood, chops and steaks. Homemade potato chips are a bar standard, and the bread, focaccia and pizza are excellent. The menu changes frequently and features local, seasonal, healthy foods, expertly prepared. Save room for dessert—Three Little Custards, L.A. Ice, Chocolate Cake with Door County Cherries, or Tennessee Ice Cream Sundae. During the season, enjoy eating on our outdoor terrace.

Parking: Free underground parking after 4:00 p.m., and all day on the weekends. Enter from West Wilson Street.

L.A. ICE

Inspired by the work of Tandem Press artist, Gronk.

2   cups fresh lime juice
3   cups fresh orange juice
4   tablespoons fresh lemon juice
      Dash of salt
½   ounce Tequila
1   jigger Gran Torres Orange Liqueur
1   cup simple syrup
      Additional Gran Torres Orange Liqueur

Combine all ingredients in a shallow plastic or stainless steel pan—do not use glass or aluminum. The syrup should be at least 1 inch high. Cover and let freeze until hard (15-20 hours).

To serve, scrape an ice cream scoop along the top in long strokes to "gather" the scoop of ice. Pour 1 additional teaspoon Gran Torres over the top of each serving.

Yields 10 servings

THE WISCONSIN ROOM

The Wisconsin Room of The American Club
Highland Drive
Kohler, Wisconsin 53044
414-457-8000

Open Monday through Saturday
6:00 a.m. to 2:00 p.m.

Sunday 10:00 a.m. to 2:00 p.m.

Daily for dinner 5:00 p.m. to 9:00 p.m.

All major credit cards accepted

The Wisconsin Room is The American Club's original dining hall, located in the hotel's historic wing. Refurbished in 1993, the room provides seating for up to 140 people. Oak paneling, antique chandeliers, leaded glass windows, elegant floral print draperies, and fine furniture pieces by Baker are distinguishing aspects of the interior design. Two large Wisconsin-theme tapestries commissioned in the 1940s adorn its walls, and drawings of distinguished Wisconsinites line its entry corridor. Another tribute to the Wisconsin Room's historic past is the carefully preserved leaded glass panels above the French doors that face the hotel's English garden courtyard. The panels show the Kohler Co. medallion and motto, and a John Ruskin quote that was a favorite of American Club founder, Walter J. Kohler, Sr.: "Life without labor is guilt, labor without art is brutality." For warm-weather entertaining, The Wisconsin Room features two private dining terraces. Breakfast and dinner are served in The Wisconsin Room daily; Sunday brunch is also a Wisconsin Room tradition, as are seasonal holiday dinners.

WISCONSIN CHEESE & CLAM CROSTINI

*Ideal as an appetizer—convenient to serve and eat, and easy to personalize
with your own variations—crostini are also superb accompaniments
to main courses, such as an entree salad or a hearty omelette.*

1/2	cup Wisconsin butter
1	teaspoon finely chopped garlic, divided
2	24-inch French bread loaves, cut horizontally into 2 pieces
1/4	pound apple-smoked bacon
1	cup finely diced onions
1	cup cooked chopped sea clams
1	cup finely diced red, yellow, green peppers
1/2	cup bread crumbs
2	tablespoons finely chopped basil
1/2	cup grated fresh Wisconsin Parmesan cheese
1/2	cup grated Wisconsin Mozzarella cheese
1/2	cup grated Wisconsin Pepato cheese (Romano with peppercorns)

Melt butter in a small sauce pot; add half of the garlic, cook 1 minute and remove
from heat. Brush bread with garlic butter and reserve for later.

Dice apple-smoked bacon and render in large saute pan until crispy. Add onions and
saute over medium heat until tender, approximately 2-3 minutes.

Add remaining garlic, clams and peppers and saute until heated through. Remove
from heat and stir in bread crumbs and basil; allow to cool. Place in 4-quart bowl and stir
in grated cheeses. Divide mixture evenly over each half of French bread.

Bake open-faced loaves in a 350-degree oven on a large cookie sheet until crisp.
Slice on the diagonal into 1-inch thick pieces and serve hot.

Yields 6-8 servings

INDEX OF RECIPES